TOTAL BAR
AND BEVERAGE
MANAGEMENT

TOTAL BAR AND BEVERAGE MANAGEMENT

Philip Moore

Lebhar-Friedman Books
Chain Store Publishing Corp.
A Subsidiary of Lebhar-Friedman, Inc.
New York

CONTENTS

TOTAL BAR
AND BEVERAGE
MANAGEMENT

Chapter 1

PURCHASING

The wholesale pricing of alcoholic beverages is rigidly controlled through state laws and, as a result, there is no negotiating of price involved. Yet, nevertheless, a buyer who has a keen awareness of state laws and a thorough understanding of the fundamental concepts of liquor purchasing will benefit considerably. Unfortunately, because the various state laws differ so radically and are altered so often, it would simply not be feasible to explore them in any detail within this book. Therefore, the goal of this section will be to examine those common fundamental concepts which will serve as the foundation to the building of a sound purchasing program.

The course of study can be categorized into four sections, liquor purchasing, wine purchasing, beer purchasing, and bar supply purchasing.

LIQUOR PURCHASING
Wholesale Liquor Distributors

In most states, the purchasing of alcoholic beverages is done through dealing with a number of wholesale liquor distributors. Each of these distributors will normally offer a wide variety of liquors and a small number of "exclusive" liquors, those handled by no other distributor in the area. As a result of each distributor having a limited number of exclusive items, a buyer who wishes to stock a full line of liquor will be forced to deal with a large number of distributors.

1

As an aid in recalling the items handled by each distributor, the buyer should construct a distributor sheet, similar to the example sheet in Figure 1. Notice in the example that a number of items are handled by a variety of distributors, while other items are handled by one exclusively.

In a small number of states, the state itself performs the duties of the wholesale liquor distributor. In those states, privately owned liquor distributors are forbidden to operate, and buyers are required to deal only with the state.

The laws and company policies which dictate the actual steps involved in ordering and receiving liquor (minimum purchase requirements, time lapse before delivery, billing dates, penalties, late charges, etc.) differ considerably among the states, but they are critically important and must be thoroughly understood by the buyer.

Mathematics of Liquor Purchasing

Five general factors can affect the wholesale cost of a bottle of liquor. None of the factors are complicated, but a buyer must be aware of each in order to make sound purchasing decisions. The factors to consider are the basic discount structure, assortment purchasing discounts, post off discounts, size price variations, and open case costs.

Basic Discount Structures

In an effort to influence buyers to purchase in larger quantities, liquor distributors extend volume-related discounts. An example of such a discount structure is illustrated below.

	Size	List	5cs	10cs	15cs	25cs
Brand X						
Bourbon	qt	66.00	−3.00	−6.00	—	−9.00

The example indicates that one case of Brand X Bourbon, quarts, would cost the buyer $66.00, but the distributor will offer a three dollar per case discount if five cases are purchased, a six dollar per case discount if ten cases are purchased and a nine dollar per case discount if twenty-five cases are purchased.

When analyzing the discount rates on a cost-per-quart basis, the example can be broken down as follows:

Amount of Purchase	Case and Unit Costs		
1 to 4 cases	Case Cost	=	$66.00
	Quart Cost	=	$66.00 \div 12$
		=	$5.50
5 to 9 cases	Case Cost	=	$66.00 - $3.00
		=	$63.00
	Quart Cost	=	$63.00 \div 12$
		=	$5.25
10 to 24 cases	Case Cost	=	$66.00 - $6.00
		=	$60.00
	Quart Cost	=	$60.00 \div 12$
		=	$5.00
25 cases and over	Case Cost	=	$66.00 - $9.00
		=	$57.00
	Quart Cost	=	$57.00 \div 12$
		=	$4.75

The basic discount structure can vary radically with each brand of liquor. Some liquors have discounts available at two cases, while others will start at three cases, and still others have no discounts until five cases are purchased. Some brands of liquor have minimal or even no discounts, while others offer the buyer tremendous savings through extensive discount rates.

With these thoughts in mind, it should be obvious that a buyer must study and compare discount rates as well as list prices. Often it will be better to purchase an item with a higher list price because the item offers a better discount rate. An example of such a situation is illustrated below.

	Size	List	2cs	5cs	10cs
Brand A Rum	qt	58.00	—	−4.00	−5.00
Brand B Rum	qt	60.00	−5.00	−5.50	−6.00

SAMPLE DISTRIBUTOR SHEET

	Southern	Youngs	NDC	Don Snyder	Simon Levi	William George	Western
AMERICAN WHISKEY							
Early Times					▓	▓	
Fleischmann's				▓			
I. W. Harper	▓						
Jack Daniel's		▓			▓		
Jim Beam				▓			▓
Old Grand Dad			▓				
Old Overholt			▓				
Old Taylor			▓				
Seagram's 7 Crown							▓
CANADIAN WHISKY							
Canadian Club			▓				
Crown Royal							▓
Seagram's V.O.							▓
SCOTCH WHISKY							
Ballantine's		▓				▓	
Black & White		▓					
Catto's				▓	▓		
Chivas Regal					▓		
Cutty Sark	▓	▓				▓	
Dewar's	▓						
J & B				▓	▓		
Johnnie Walker Black				▓			▓
Johnnie Walker Red				▓			▓
IRISH WHISKEY							
Murphey's				▓			▓
Old Bushmills		▓	▓	▓	▓	▓	▓
TEQUILA							
Jose Cuervo Gold	▓	▓				▓	▓
Jose Cuervo 1800	▓	▓				▓	▓
Pepe Lopez					▓		
GIN							
Beefeater		▓					
Bombay				▓	▓		
Fleischmann's	▓			▓			
Tanqueray				▓			▓
VODKA							
Fleischmann's				▓			
Smirnoff		▓					
Stolichnaya			▓	▓			

FIGURE 1

SAMPLE DISTRIBUTOR SHEET (Cont.)

	Southern	Youngs	NDC	Don Snyder	Simon Levi	William George	Western
RUM							
Bacardi Amber		■				■	
Bacardi Silver		■				■	
Bacardi 151		■				■	
Myer's							■
Trigo				■			
BRANDY—COGNAC							
Christian Brothers		■				■	
Paul Masson				■			■
Courvoisier			■				
Hennessey	■		■				
Martell	■	■		■	■	■	
Remy Martin	■				■		
LIQUEURS							
Amaretto Di Saronno					■		
B & B		■				■	
Benedictine		■				■	
Drambuie			■				
Galliano		■			■	■	■
Kahlua	■	■		■	■	■	■
Metaxa					■		
Tuaca					■		
Strega	■						
CORDIALS (Bols)							
Anisette					■		
Blackberry Brandy					■		
Cacao—Dark					■		
Cacao—White					■		
Cherry Brandy					■		
Creme de Banana					■		
Creme de Cassis					■		
Creme de Noyaux					■		
Creme de Menthe—Green					■		
Creme de Menthe—White					■		

From the standpoint of list price (the price of one case), Brand A rum is the less expensive, but, due to the effect of the discount rates, when buying in lots of two, three, or four cases, Brand B is $3.00 per case less expensive.

Analyzing further, the buyer will find that when five or more cases of rum are purchased Brand A will again become less expensive than Brand B rum.

Therefore, from the standpoint of cost, Brand B rum will be the better value when purchasing two, three, or four cases, and Brand A rum will be the better value in all other instances.

Post Off Discounts

Periodically, for merchandising purposes, a distributor might elect to reduce the price of a particular brand of liquor. The amount of the price reduction, which is commonly referred to as the "post off" discount, is either taken directly off the list price or added to the basic discount rate.

For example, if Brand X scotch with a $65.00 list price, is announced to be $5.00 per case post off, the list price would change to $60.00 and the discount rate would remain the same. Therefore, if five cases of Brand X scotch were purchased, the cost of each case would be $57.00.

	Size	List	5cs	10cs	15cs	25cs
Brand X						
Scotch	qt	65.00	−3.00	−8.25	—	−9.00

Sometimes the post off rate will be added to the discount rates rather than the list price. For example, Brand X scotch might be post off eight dollars when purchased in lots of five cases, instead of three dollars. In such an instance the list price will remain the same and the benefit of the post off discount will only be realized if five to nine cases are purchased.

Post off rates usually last only a short time, and they are usually announced at least two weeks prior to taking effect. As a result, it's imperative that the buyer keep well abreast of the changing post off discounts and gear purchasing accordingly.

Size Variations

The cost of an ounce of liquor will sometimes vary with the size of the bottle purchased. For example, in the illustration below, Brand X bourbon is sold by the quart, fifth, pint, and half gallon.

BRAND X — Straight Bourbon Whiskey — 86°
Quarts   4.56
Fifths   3.78
Pints   2.34
1/2 Gal. 8.83

The cost per ounce of each size is as follows:

Quarts = 4.56/32   = 14.25¢ per ounce
Fifths = 3.78/25.6 = 14.77¢ per ounce
Pints = 2.34/16   = 14.62¢ per ounce
½ Gal. = 8.83/64   = 13.80¢ per ounce

If a bar manager changed from quarts to half gallons in an effort to save money, the following savings would be realized:

Savings per ounce = 14.25 − 13.80 = .45¢
Savings per quart = .45 × 32   = 14.4¢
Savings per case = 14.4 × 12   = $1.73

Because the savings are only minimal, a decision would have to be made as to whether the change would be worth the inconvenience imposed on the bartenders. Half gallon sizes are obviously larger and heavier, and as a result are more difficult to work with.

In this particular example, the decision would probably be to stay with the more convenient quart sizes, but what if it were announced that half gallons of Brand X bourbon were post off ten dollars per case from the list price? Now the total savings per case would be $11.73 and the change might be a wise decision.

Another factor for the buyer to consider is the basic discount rate associated with each size. In the previous example, comparing the quarts to half gallons of Brand X bourbon, the basic discount structures might look like this:

	Size	List	3cs	5cs	10cs	25cs
Brand X						
Bourbon	qt	54.72	−4.75	−5.00	−7.50	−9.00
Brand X						
Bourbon	½ gl	52.98	−1.00	−1.50	−2.00	−3.00

In this case, the buyer can receive far better discounts when buying Brand X bourbon in quarts, as opposed to half gallons. In fact, when purchasing three cases, the cost per ounce is actually lower when buying quarts. Therefore, unless a substantially large post off discount was given to the half gallon size, there would be no comparison between the two, and the buyer would always purchase Brand X bourbon in quarts.

Often, when comparing the cost per ounce of two bottle sizes, a buyer will have to compare liters to quarts, or milliliters to liters. To simplify the process, the following conversions should be used:

$$1.75 \text{ liters} = \text{approximately } 59.18 \text{ ounces}$$
$$1 \text{ liter} = \text{approximately } 33.81 \text{ ounces}$$
$$750 \text{ milliliters} = \text{approximately } 25.36 \text{ ounces}$$
$$200 \text{ milliliters} = \text{approximately } 6.76 \text{ ounces}$$

$$1 \text{ gallon} = 128 \text{ ounces}$$
$$\text{½ gallon} = 64 \text{ ounces}$$
$$1 \text{ quart} = 32 \text{ ounces}$$
$$1 \text{ fifth} = 25.6 \text{ ounces}$$
$$1 \text{ pint} = 16 \text{ ounces}$$
$$1 \text{ tenth} = 12.8 \text{ ounces}$$

Using these conversions, the cost per ounce of each of the various sizes of Brand A gin can be calculated as follows:

BRAND A—Gin

Quarts	8.63
750 ml	6.94
Tenth	3.68
200 ml	2.10
175 L	15.00

Quarts = 8.63/32 = 26.97¢ per ounce
750 ml = 6.94/25.36 = 27.37¢ per ounce
Tenth = 3.68/12.8 = 28.75¢ per ounce
200 ml = 2.10/6.76 = 31.07¢ per ounce
175 L = 15.00/59.18 = 25.35¢ per ounce

Assortment Discount Structures

The assortment discount structure, sometimes referred to as the multiple brands discount structure, is a simple variation of the basic discount structure. It's offered as a means of influencing a buyer to purchase an assortment of items available from a single distiller or importer. This should not be confused with a single *distributor,* it is the *distiller* or *importer* who will offer the assortment discount.

Assortment discounting can be explained as follows; a buyer can purchase cases of a variety of liquors from the same distiller or importer and use the *total assorted case count* to determine the individual rate of discount for *each brand.*

In the example below, Acme distillers offers an assortment discount on Brand A vodka, Brand B bourbon, Brand C gin, and Brand D rum.

ACME DISTILLERS

	Size	List	5cs	10cs	15cs	25cs
Brand A Vodka	qt	51.50	− 5.00	− 5.50	—	− 8.50
Brand B Bourbon	qt	62.90	− 3.50	− 4.50	− 5.00	− 7.00
Brand C Gin	qt	57.25	− 3.00	− 4.50	—	—
Brand D Rum	qt	52.00	− 2.00	− 3.00	—	− 5.00

If a buyer elected to purchase only three cases of Brand A vodka and one case of Brand B bourbon, the total purchase would be four cases and the buyer would pay full list price for each item, but if the buyer added one case of Brand D rum, the purchase would total five cases and, because all of the items assort for discount, the buyer would receive a five case discount on each item.

The cost of the purchase would be derived as follows:

	List	5cs Discount			Cases Purchased		Total Cost
Brand A							
Vodka	51.50	−	5.00	= 46.50 ×	3	=	$139.50
Brand B							
Bourbon	62.90	−	3.50	= 59.40 ×	1	=	59.40
Brand D							
Rum	52.00	−	2.00	= 50.00 ×	1	=	50.00
				Total cost of Purchase		=	$248.90

Assortment discounts can offer the astute buyer substantial savings. Even in the small purchase illustrated in the example the buyer realized a $20.50 savings off the list price. When buying in large quantities the savings could easily amount to several hundred dollars over a period of only one month.

The proper use of assortment discounts is a key factor in a sound liquor purchasing program.

Open Case Costs

To influence buyers to purchase in cases, as opposed to single bottles, distributing companies will usually charge an open case cost for each single bottle purchased. This cost will only be in the area of ten cents, but it will be added to the cost of each bottle.

Although the charge is small, it will, when added to the cost of a large number of items over a period of time, amount to a total that the buyer should be aware of.

Each of these five cost influencing factors have been outlined in a very general manner. Detailed laws associated with each will vary considerably from state to state and must be investigated by the buyer before they can be put to use.

Purchasing Economics

In most states, a buyer will usually be granted a short period of time after receiving a delivery of liquor before the payment for it becomes due. If that period happens to be 30 days, and if the buyer always purchases only enough liquor to last 30 days, the buyer would enjoy a 100 percent cash flow situation. This means the buyer would never have to invest added money, because each liquor bill would be paid with a portion of the revenue received from the sale of that liquor.

If, on the other hand, in an effort to take advantage of volume discounts, the same buyer were to purchase enough liquor to last 90 days, there would have to be an added investment made. Each bottle would be purchased at a reduced rate, due to the discount, but there will be capital tied up in liquor inventory that will not be fully released until 60 days after the bill is paid.

The buyer must now answer the question of whether the added discount is worth the added investment, which brings us to the economics of purchasing, or the analysis of purchasing from an investment standpoint.

The answer to any such question is dependent upon three factors:

1) The amount of discount received
2) The amount of capital invested
3) The rate of inventory turnover

Knowing these factors, a buyer can compute an *average percentage rate of return* on the investment, and based on that percentage make a logical decision.

In the example below a buyer has to make a decision on well vodka. The *rate of turnover* (the rate of sales) of the vodka is five cases each 30 days. As a result, the buyer has been purchasing the vodka every 30 days, and enjoying both a five case discount and a 100 percent cash flow situation. Now a post off discount of $10.00 per case when purchased at 15 cases, has been announced for Brand X vodka and the buyer has to decide whether or not to take advantage of the discount.

	Size	List	5cs	10cs	15cs
Brand X					
Vodka	qt	$51.50	− 5.00	—	− 10.00

Rate of turnover: 5 cases each 30 days

Each of the options should be reviewed separately, as follows:

5 Case Purchase:

Case Purchase Price: $51.50 − $5.00 = $46.50

Cash Investment: 0

(Remember, when the bill comes due all of the vodka will have been sold and, therefore, the bill would be paid with a portion of the revenue. No extra cash investment would have to be made.)

15 Case Purchase:

Case Purchase Price: $51.50 − $10.00 = $41.50

Cash Investment: $415.00

Length of Investment: 60 days

(The actual cost of the purchase would be $622.50, but if the bill were paid 30 days after delivery only 10 cases would still be remaining. 10 × $41.50 = $415.00)

Therefore, when purchasing 15 cases the buyer would realize a savings of $75.00 (5.00 per case × 15 cases), but to receive that savings a $415.00 investment would have to be made over a period of 60 days. Even though the buyer would be purchasing enough vodka to last 90 days, the actual investment would not be made until the billing date, 30 days after the delivery. As a result, the investment would only occur during the final 60 days of the 90 day period.

The final, and most overlooked factor to consider is that the entire $415.00 is not tied up for the entire 60 day period. Throughout that period the vodka will continue to sell, and therefore, the buyer will realize a continual return on the investment. This point is well illustrated in the graph in Figure 2.

Because the actual amount of capital tied up in Brand X vodka will be decreasing on a daily basis, the buyer must view the total investment in terms of an *average amount* as opposed to a set amount. Because the investment capital will be returned at a relatively steady rate, the *average investment* can easily be derived by dividing the initial investment in half, as illustrated in the graph in Figure 3.

The *average percentage rate of return* can then be easily calculated using the following formula:

$$\frac{\text{Total Savings}}{\text{Average Investment}} = \begin{array}{l}\text{Average Percentage Rate of Return}\\\text{Throughout the investment period}\end{array}$$

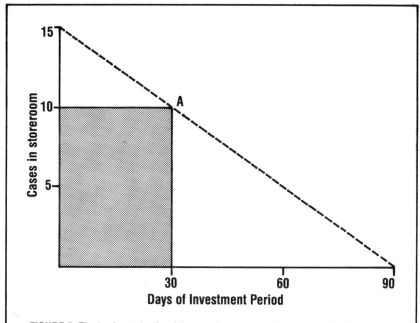

FIGURE 2: The horizontal axis of the graph represents the days of the investment period, while the vertical axis represents the cases of Brand X vodka remaining in the storeroom. The dotted line represents the inventory of Brand X vodka at various points throughout the investment period.

Notice that the inventory is continually dropping. After 30 days, when the bill is actually paid, there are only ten cases remaining in the storeroom, as noted at point A.

FIGURE 2

The *average percentage rate of return* for the example investment would be:

$$\frac{\$75.00}{\$415.00/2} = \frac{75}{207.50} = \quad 36.14\% \text{ throughout the 60 day period.}$$

Even though the 36.14 percent is only an average rate of return in this example, when making investment comparisons the buyer should consider this figure to be the true 60 day rate of return on the investment.

If the buyer wished to determine the rate of return on an annual basis, the following formula would be used:

$$\begin{array}{ccc} \text{Annual Average Percentage} & = & \text{Average Percentage} \times \dfrac{365}{\text{Days of Investment}} \\ \text{Rate of Return} & & \text{Rate of Return} \end{array}$$

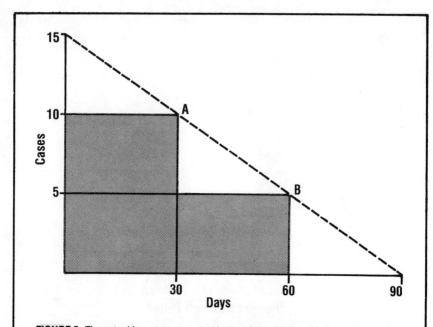

FIGURE 3: The actual investment period is the 60 days located between the 30 day and 90 day points on the graph. Because the storeroom inventory will be dropping at a relatively constant rate, the average inventory figure will be located at the median point of the investment period. On this graph the median point of the investment period would occur 60 days after the delivery, point B on the graph, at which time there are five cases remaining in the storeroom. The cost of those five cases would equal the average investment over the 60 day period.
Because the storeroom inventory will be proportionate to the remaining time in the investment period, the average investment could be determined by simply dividing the original investment in half.

FIGURE 3

The *annual average percentage rate of return* realized in the example investment would be determined as follows:

$$36.14 \times \frac{365}{60} = 36.14 \times 6.083 = \underline{219.84\%}$$

When making a comparative analysis of the average percentage rate of return between two liquor investments the buyer must be certain that the rates are based on identical time periods. This is best done by analyzing all investments on an annual basis.

For example, if the buyer in our example were also considering a twenty-five case purchase, which happened to yield a thirteen dollar per case discount, the purchase would be analyzed as follows:

> 25 Case Purchase
> Case Purchase Price: $51.50 − $13.00 = $38.50
> Cash Investment: $770.00 ($38.50 × 20 cases)
> Length of Investment: 120 Days

Therefore, when purchasing 25 cases the buyer would realize a savings of $200.00 ($8.00 per case × 25 cases) over the cost of purchasing five cases at a time, but would have to make an initial investment of $770.00.

The average percentage rate of return over the 120 day investment period would be calculated as follows:

$$\frac{\$200.00}{\$770.00/2} = \frac{200.00}{385.00} = \underline{51.95\%}$$

Notice that the average percentage rate of return is higher than that in a ten case purchase (51.95 percent vs. 36.14 percent), but these figures are deceiving because the investment periods are not identical (120 days vs. 60 days). Therefore, the buyer should make a true comparison by viewing both purchases on an *annual average percentage rate of return.*

The *annual average percentage rate of return* on the 25 case purchase would be calculated as follows:

$$51.95 \times \frac{365}{120} = 51.95 \times 3.042 = \underline{158.03\%}$$

Therefore, on an annual basis, the average percentage rate of return is better on a ten case purchase than on a 25 case purchase (158.03 percent vs. 219.84 percent). The total savings will be greater when purchasing 25 cases at a time, but the investment made to realize those savings will be proportionately greater than the investment made to realize the savings associated with a ten case purchase.

It is always best to have all investment capital yielding the highest possible annual average percentage rate of return. Therefore, the buyer in the example illustration should elect to purchase Brand X vodka in ten case lots, and utilize the remaining investment capital in other situations.

Establishing a Purchasing Program

It is a highly desirable policy for the buyer to establish a definite purchasing schedule. Whether the purchasing is to be done at the first of each month or on every other Monday is of no importance, as long as that pattern is consistently adhered to.

By implementing such a schedule, the buyer can be assured that all of the deliveries will be made on the same day. As a result, all of the liquor will be stored and all of the adjustments on the perpetual inventory system will be noted on the same day. For the purpose of inventory control, this one day process is far superior to the practice of receiving deliveries on a sporadic basis.

Having a purchasing schedule also makes billing procedures easier. When all orders are delivered on the same day, all bills will become due on the same day and, therefore, bookkeeping can be simplified.

Finally, when restricted to purchasing only on selected days, the buyer will be forced to check each brand in the entire liquor inventory; as a result, the possibility of running out of a brand of liquor due to the buyer's oversight will be greatly reduced.

In any aspect of purchasing, it is always a good policy to keep a written record of all orders. When this is done, the person receiving deliveries can immediately verify their accuracy through checking the ordering form. Figure 4 is a simple example of such a form. When writing the order, the buyer should clarify the quantity ordered, the specific bottle sizes, and, when applicable, the proof.

Working with Salespeople

Each distributor will usually be represented by a staff of sales representatives who will call on each buyer in their respective areas on a regular basis. The buyer who deals with these salespeople properly will find them to be a valuable asset.

Once a purchasing schedule has been established and definite purchasing dates have been set, the buyer should next make arrangements to meet with

LIQUOR ORDERING FORM

Date	Distributor	Order:
¹¹/₁₇	WESTERN	3cs. 7 CROWN (QTS) 6 ONLY JIM BEAM (QTS) 3cs. VO. (QTS) 1 cs. KAHLUA (1.75 LTR)
¹¹/₁₇	SNYDER	9cs FLEISCHMANN'S VODKA (LTR) 5cs. CATTO'S SCOTCH(CT) 3cs FLEISCHMANN'S GIN (LTR) 3cs FLEISCHMANN'S WHISKEY (LTR)
¹¹/₁₇	YOUNGS	1 cs. BEEFEATER (1.75 LTR) 1 cs. SMIRNOFF (QTS) 1cs CUTTY SARK (1.75 LTR) 6 ONLY BALLANTINES (QTS)
¹¹/₁₇	NDC	1 cs. CANADIAN CLUB (QTS) 6 ONLY COURVOISIER (FIFTHS) 4 ONLY DRAMBUIE (FIFTHS)
¹¹/₁₇	SIMON LEVI	6 ONLY MARTELL (FIFTHS) 2 ONLY REMY MARTIN (FIFTHS) 2 ONLY TUACA (FIFTHS) 6 ONLY EARLY TIMES (QTS)

FIGURE 4

each sales representative on those dates. A specific time schedule, based on the buyer's convenience, should also be established.

The buyer should request that each salesperson present all coming changes in both list prices and discount rates, and introduce all new items on those days.

Besides keeping the buyer well informed on all price variations, salesreps can also be a valuable aid to the buyer in rectifying shipping problems, purchasing errors, and billing mistakes.

Selecting Well Liquor

The primary objective in selecting well liquors should be customer satisfaction, in terms of both price and quality. Quality should be emphasized in every aspect of a bar operation, but with regards to the selection of the brands of well liquor it need not be overemphasized. The astute buyer will always remember the following:

1) Very few customers will actually inquire as to the brands of well liquor.

2) Those who order well drinks are, for the most part, either indifferent to taste or primarily concerned with price.
3) Those customers who are very sensitive to taste will normally order a specific brand of call liquor instead of well liquor.
4) Quite often the quality of well liquor will be indetectable, due to being either mixed or blended with cream, fruit juices, or carbonated mixes.

Therefore, the first goal should be to select well liquor which can, from a business standpoint, be sold at a price acceptable to customers. Because well items will be purchased in case lots, strong emphasis should be placed on their basic and assortment discount rates.

Quality should be viewed in terms of local popularity, which will vary considerably throughout the country. A survey should be made of well brands of competitive establishments and sales representatives should be asked about local sales trends. A final decision should never be made before each brand has been tested and a positive customer response registered.

A number of medium- to lower-priced establishments have experimented with the idea of pouring expensive brands of liquor in their wells, in an effort to increase sales. The results have usually been unfavorable, because management normally makes the critical mistake of trying to immediately recoup their added expense through increasing prices. As a result, instead of offering customers more quality for the same price, they've, in a sense, eliminated their well liquors and forced their customers to drink and pay for call liquors.

A successful buyer will never lose sight of the fact that call liquors and well liquors must be both categorized and thought of in separate terms. The manner in which each is purchased and the manner in which each is priced will be critical to the success of the establishment.

The only exception to the rule of considering price first occurs when purchasing for very expensive, high quality restaurants. The clientele of such restaurants will be primarily concerned with quality in both food and beverage, and price will be very secondary in importance. Therefore, by pouring expensive, high quality liquors in their well, such restaurants will both project prestige and add to the enjoyment of their customers' dining experience. Even from a business standpoint this policy will prove sound, because the added expenses can easily be compensated for through increased cocktail prices, without offending customers. Those who patronize such establishments expect to pay a high price, because they expect the finest in quality.

Selecting Call Liquors and Liqueurs

The specific variety of call liquors and liqueurs that a buyer should purchase will be dependent upon the goals of the establishment and the preferences of the clientele. The only rule that can be applied to all bars is "if it sells, stock it, if it doesn't, don't."

The goal of the buyer should be to avoid needlessly tying up capital in brands of liquors which do not sell. Generally speaking, any bottle of liquor which does not turn over within eight weeks should be discontinued.

Fortunately, management can quickly recoup their investments in such liquors by simply converting them to well liquors. Certainly, the return will not be as great as it would have been if the item were sold at call prices, but the return will be immediate and a profit will still be realized. This policy is far superior to the alternative of leaving the investment to sit on a storeroom shelf for an indefinite period of time.

Unfortunately, when dealing with liqueurs management will be unable to consider this alternative. Therefore, restraint should be exercised when purchasing all but the most traditionally popular liqueurs. Newly introduced liqueurs are usually a particularly bad investment, unless they are backed by an exceptionally strong advertising campaign, which is seldom the case.

Customer preferences differ considerably throughout the country, and to a lesser extent they will differ from bar to bar within the same area. Preferences will also change as the seasons change and as popular drinking trends change. Therefore, management must continually stay aware of customer requests and maintain a constant policy of both adding new brands of requested liquors and dropping brands of liquor that sell poorly.

The only exception to the rule of dropping exceptionally slow moving liquors again occurs when purchasing for a very high quality oriented restaurant, a restaurant which specializes in offering its customers a full service dining experience. To such a restaurant the added investment involved in carrying an extremely large variety of liquors is a necessity in maintaining their image.

WINE PURCHASING

The actual mechanics involved in purchasing wine are very similar to those of purchasing liquor. The factors governing bottle cost and purchasing economics are, for the most part, identical to those associated with purchasing liquor, and individual state laws also control the wholesale distribution of wine.

Although there are distributors who deal exclusively with wine, the majority of liquor distributors also handle wine. These liquor distributors normally employ specialized sales representatives who deal only with wine, and who will be of great value to the buyer in the evaluation of wines, while the regular sales representative will keep the buyer abreast of both wine and liquor price variations on a regular basis.

Wine purchasing can be categorized into two areas: bottled wines and house wines.

Bottled Wines

When purchasing bottled wines, the buyer should give special consideration to both storage facilities and the actual selection of inventory.

Storage Facilities

Every bottled wine must be stored on its side, to keep the cork moist and expanded. Otherwise, the cork will dry and, as a result, shrink, allowing air to enter the bottle and eventually spoil the wine. If specially constructed wine racks are not available, the wines may be stored within their delivery cases, stacked in a manner which will allow the bottles to remain horizontal. Unfortunately a number of wine cases will consume a large amount of space, especially within a refrigeration unit.

Wines should be stored at a stable temperature, preferably between 55 and 60 degrees. Because white, rose, and sparkling wines must be served cold, there must be enough refrigeration space available to store ample amounts of all chilled wines to guarantee immediate service.

Whether the wine is stored at the bar and issued by the bartender or in a separate storage area and issued by the floor manager is of little importance. What is very important is that there be proper storage space for every wine on the wine list. The variety of wines purchased should only be as large as the storage areas permit.

Inventory Selection

A comparative analysis of wine vineyards, vintages, or varieties is an extremely involved and highly personal subject. The subject is actually an entire field of study within itself, and would be impossible to do justice to within this book.

There are, however, a number of business-related factors that a buyer must first consider before reaching the point of a comparative taste analysis.

The Menu

It is best for the buyer to consider wine as a food rather than a liquor. The wine list should be thought of as an extension of the food menu in terms of quality, price, and length of selection.

It is important for the buyer to remember that the great majority of customers base their selection of a restaurant on the quality and price range of the food. Therefore the buyer must select a wine list which will be acceptable to the specific clientele of the restaurant; the list may therefore, especially in the less expensive restaurants, differ considerably from what might be acceptable to a wine connoisseur.

Popularity Versus Quality

As a general rule, a popular, well advertised wine will far outsell a less expensive yet better quality wine which either bears an uncommon name or is produced in one of the lesser known vineyards. It is very important that the buyer not lose sight of this fact during comparative tastings. From a business standpoint, priority importance must be given to what will sell, not necessarily what tastes best.

Wholesale Cost

As the popularity of wines grows in the United States, so does customer awareness of retail prices. A buyer can no longer establish prices by simply using a standard markup policy such as three times the wholesale price. Customers now often become offended when asked to pay prices which are sometimes well over twice the amount they pay at the store.

The buyer cannot, however, afford to eliminate those very popular wines from the wine list simply because their wholesale prices will not allow for a standard markup. Because of their popularity it is very important that these wines stay on the list, and to ensure steady sales the buyer will simply have to create a more conservative markup policy. As the old saying goes, "You can't bank percentages!"

The Number of Selections

Finer restaurants, which feature a wide variety of specially prepared foods, will normally offer their customers an extensive variety of wines to choose from. They use the wine list as a means of promoting the excellence and completeness of the service of their establishment, by giving customers an opportunity to perfectly complement their meal with their exact preference of wine.

For these restaurants, an extensive wine list is imperative, if for no other reason than to give credibility to their claims of excellence. An exceptional dining experience requires not only a balance of fine foods, but also a perfectly compatible beverage. The choice of the perfect beverage can only be determined by the customer, who should be offered a wide variety of wines to choose from.

These restaurants will find the cost involved in stocking such a large inventory well worth the prestige that a lengthy wine selection will generate. After all, it is prestige that these restaurants are selling and prestige that allows them to charge exorbitant prices without offending their customers.

On the other hand, less expensive establishments are normally better off limiting the size of their wine inventory. A smaller variety is easier to control, easier to properly store, and will turn over at a faster rate. In fact, a number of restaurateurs who specialize in medium-priced restaurants have stated that after reducing the number of selections on their wine lists their wine sales have actually increased. They say that longer wine lists had the effect of confusing some of their customers, while it was bad from a psychological standpoint for others, in that it forced them to make a difficult decision between a large number of wines. By lowering the number of red wines, for example, from twenty to five, many of the less knowledgeable customers were not so intimidated and felt more at ease in making a selection. These restaurateurs say that the small number of sales lost due to the elimination of the less popular wines were easily made up by implementing creative merchandising techniques—less costly and easier to control than an extensive wine list.

Yet even though these arguments seem logical, some restaurateurs insist that only since they have increased the number of wines on their lists have they realized increased sales.

Exactly how large of a variety of bottled wines a medium- to lower-priced restaurant should stock may be debatable, but the actual number is not nearly as important as the wines themselves. The buyer must base the selections strictly on the preferences of the specific clientele of the restaurant. The customers should be offered both a selection they're familiar with and a price they can afford.

House Wines

House wines, often referred to as jug or bulk wines because they are usually purchased in gallon containers, bear the same relationship to bottled wines that well liquors have to call liquors. The primary considerations in the selection of house wines are identical to those used in the selection of well liquors; customer satisfaction in price and customer satisfaction in quality.

There are usually only three house wines: one red, one white, and one rose, and they are normally all the same brand.

Before making a final decision on a particular brand of house wine, the buyer should remember the following:

1) Only a small percentage of customers will actually inquire as to the brand of house wine.

2) Those who order, for example, red wine by the liter or half liter, as opposed to selecting a specific bottled red wine by the fifth or tenth, are normally more concerned with price than extraordinary flavor.

3) Customers who are particularly sensitive about the quality of their wine will normally select a specific bottled wine, rather than a house wine.

Just as with well liquor, the buyer's first goal should be to select a house wine that can, from a business standpoint, be sold at a price acceptable to customers. This is not to say that quality should be overlooked, which should never be the case. Yet regardless of the quality of wine selected, the price to the customers should remain relatively low.

Determining the Value of Quality

Too often buyers base their selections of house wines on the assumption that the customers will consider the quality of the house wine to be a direct reflection on the quality of the restaurant. As a result, buyers often consider quality first and price second. This is not necessarily a bad policy, if the restaurant intends to absorb the added cost. The more prestigious reputation may indeed impress a small percentage of customers, while the finer taste should result in increased sales.

If, on the other hand, the buyer intends to pass the added cost of the more expensive wine on to the customers, through increasing prices, it would probably be a mistake. The buyer must always remember that those customers who purchase house wines do so for the same reason that customers purchase well liquor, because they are more concerned with price than distinctive flavor. As a result, the buyer who improves the quality of the house wine and then forces the customers to pay for the expense will often meet with customer resentment.

As stated earlier, raising the quality of the house wine in an effort to increase sales may prove successful. The key question is, will that increase in sales be enough to offset the added purchasing cost? The buyer can better evaluate that question after determining exactly how much sales will have to increase to simply maintain the same level of gross profit currently being enjoyed using a less expensive wine. This can be done through following the steps illustrated in the example below.

All of the calculation performed in the example are derived from the following basic formulas:

$$\text{Percentage Cost (P.C.)} = \frac{\text{Cost}}{\text{Sales}}$$

$$\text{Sales} = \frac{\text{Cost}}{\text{P.C.}} = \frac{\text{Profit}}{\text{Percentage Markup}}$$

$$\text{Profit} = \text{Sales} - \text{Cost}$$

In the example, the buyer is considering increasing the quality of the house wine by switching from Brand A, which sells for $18.00 per case, to Brand B, which sells for $23.00 per case. The buyer wants to make the switch without increasing the price to the customer, but before doing so needs to determine how much the sales will have to increase to offset the added purchasing costs.

After performing the five steps illustrated below, the buyer determines that the answer is $168.05. Whether or not the added quality of wine will bring this much of an increase in sales is a decision the buyer will have to make; having an exact figure will allow the buyer to make a more realistic decision.

Actual Figures Using Brand A Wine:
    a) Customer prices based on 80% markup (20% cost)
    b) Average Monthly Usage of Brand A wines = 25 cases
    c) Cost per Case = $18.00
    d) Average Cost per Month = $18.00 × 25 = $450.00

1) What is the average monthly sales of house wine?

$$\text{Sales} = \frac{\text{Cost}}{\%\ \text{Cost}} = \frac{\$450.00}{.20} = \underline{\$2,250.00}$$

2) What is the average monthly gross profit?

$$\text{Profit} = \text{Sales} - \text{Cost} = \$2,250 - \$450 = \underline{\$1,800.00}$$

Projected Figures Based on Using Brand B Wine:
    a) Cost per Case = $23.00
    b) Average Cost per Month = $23.00 × 25 = $575.00

1) If the customer prices and total sales remain the same, what will the new house wine P.C. be?

$$\text{P.C.} = \frac{\text{Cost}}{\text{Sales}} = \frac{575}{2,250} = \underline{.2556}\ \ (25.56\%)$$

2) Given the new P.C., what will the total sales of Brand B wine have to be to yield an $1,800.00 profit?

$$\text{Sales} \quad = \quad \frac{\text{Profit}}{\% \text{ Markup}} \quad = \quad \frac{\$1,800.00}{.7444} \quad = \quad \underline{\$2,418.05}$$

(Because the P.C. equals 25.56%, the percentage markup would equal the remaining 74.44%.)

3) Using the more expensive Brand B wine, how much will the monthly sales have to increase to maintain the same level of profit currently realized using Brand A wine?

$$\$2,418.05 \quad - \quad \$2,250.00 \quad = \quad \underline{\$168.05}$$

PURCHASING BEER

Unlike liquor, beer has only a limited shelf life. This, and the fact that beer distributors usually offer little or no volume purchasing discounts, means that beer should be purchased differently than liquor and wine.

Beer should be purchased weekly, and through the use of a standard build up system. Such a system operates as follows: each brand of beer is assigned a "Build To" number and the buyer, each week, simply purchases exactly enough beer to bring the inventory level of each brand up to its assigned number. For example, if the "Build To" number of Brand X beer happened to be ten cases, and on purchasing day only two cases were remaining in the storeroom, the buyer would purchase eight cases. The Build To number refers only to the storeroom inventory, therefore, the bar should be stocked before the order is determined. Also, when counting the remaining cases, cases that are less than full should be thought of as zero inventory.

Figure 5 shows an example of a beer purchasing sheet. The number to the left of each item refers to the Build To number. The top portion of each box represents the storeroom inventory and the bottom portion represents the order. The vertical rows of boxes represent the orders for one particular week.

The Build To number should be roughly one and one half times as great as the average weekly usage. If the average weekly usage is ten cases, the Build To number should be roughly fifteen cases.

BEER PURCHASING FORM

MONTH:
DAY:

BOTTLED BEERS

	Brand "A"
	Brand "B"
	Brand "C"
	Brand "D"

DRAFT BEERS

| 2 | Brand "X" |
| 3 | Brand "Y" |

FIGURE 5

Selecting a Beer Inventory

The first factor a buyer must consider when selecting a beer inventory is refrigeration space, especially at the bar itself. For inventory control purposes, it is highly desirable to be able to store enough of each brand of beer at the bar to last through an entire day. Otherwise, the bartenders will continually be transferring beer from the storeroom to the bar. Besides being time consuming for the bartender, such a situation would greatly diminish a manager's inventory controls.

The next consideration should be customer preference. For the most part, this can be approached by stocking the two locally most popular domestic beers, the single most popular imported beer, and the single most popular light beer. This information can be obtained from beer sales representatives, but in doing so the buyer must emphasize *local* popularity. Salesreps will often try to persuade buyers with information on national sales, east coast sales, or west coast sales, but brand popularity varies widely throughout the country, therefore the buyer must base selections only on local sales records.

The third factor a buyer must analyze is the goal of the establishment. For example, a restaurant which offers only beer and wine might consider stocking a wide variety of beers and promote the extensive variety as a merchandising technique. On the other hand, restaurants which also serve liquor might elect to limit their variety of beers, and find it wiser to direct their merchandising efforts toward higher profit items such as cocktails or bottled wines.

The final decision must be made solely from a business standpoint. Before deciding to stock any brand of beer, the buyer must ask the following:

1) Is there a true customer demand for this brand of beer? Will the establishment lose business if this brand of beer is not stocked?
2) Is there enough available refrigeration space to conveniently add this brand of beer to the inventory?
3) Can this brand of beer sell at a desirable price without being merchandised? (If the answer is no, could the merchandising effort be more profitable if directed toward another area?)
4) Is stocking this beer a necessity to maintain the image of the bar or restaurant?

Rotating

As a general rule, bottled beers should be sold within 90 days of their delivery date, while keg beers should be used within 60 days. To insure freshness, management will have to see that all beers are properly rotated. All deliveries should be stored below and behind existing inventory, and when the bar is stocked in the morning the new bottles should always be stored behind the remaining bottles. Keg beers should always be stored in a row, with each delivery being placed at the end of the row.

Deposits

A deposit on the keg is always included within the price of a keg beer. As a result, the buyer should establish specifc rules regarding the storage of empty kegs. Lost or stolen kegs can add up to a considerable expense.

Bottled beers can sometimes be purchased in either returnable or non-returnable bottles. The buyer can save money through purchasing returnable bottles, but only if the great majority of the emptied bottles can be returned to the distributor. To insure this, rules will have to be established and employees will have to be taught which bottles are to be thrown away (if there are any), which bottles are to be saved, and where the saved bottles are to be stored.

BAR SUPPLY PURCHASING

All items that cannot be classified as alcoholic beverages can be grouped under the general heading of *bar supplies*. These items can be subcategorized as food items and non-food items.

All of the non-food items (glassware, napkins, straws, etc.) and a portion of the food items can be purchased from either a grocery company or, preferably, a specialized bar supply distributor. These items should be purchased on a weekly basis, through a "Build To" system, identical to that used in purchasing beer.

As the example in Figure 6 illustrates, a bar supply purchasing sheet is used in exactly the same manner as a beer purchasing sheet. The number to the left of each item represents the Build To number. The top portion of each box reflects the storeroom inventory, while the bottom portion reflects the order. The vertical rows of boxes represent the orders for one particular week.

As a general rule, the Build To number should be at least one and one half times as great as the average weekly usage. Also, because the "on hand" figure represents only the inventory remaining in the storeroom, the bar should be stocked before the order is prepared.

There should be a special section in the storeroom used exclusively for the storage of bar supplies, and each item stored within that section should be assigned an exact storage area. If possible, this area should also be used for the storage of backup supplies of glassware, because that inventory will also have to be checked on a weekly basis.

In the glassware section of the sample ordering sheet in Figure 6, the number listed below each glass denotes the code number which will be used when ordering that glass.

The perishable food items will need to be purchased from both a dairy company and a produce company, and, to insure freshness, they should be purchased at least twice each week. The purchasing should also be done

BAR SUPPLY PURCHASING SHEET

MONTH:
DAY:

FOOD PRODUCTS

Red Cherries (Jar)								
Green Cherries (Jar)								
Olives (Jar)								
Onions (Jar)								
Lime Juice (Btl)								
Grenadine (Btl)								
Sweet Sour Mix (Btl)								
Mai Tai Mix (Btl)								
Bloody Mary Mix (Btl)								
Pina Colada Mix (Btl)								
Bitters (Btl)								
Bouillion (Can)								
Orange Flower Water (Btl)								
Nutmeg (Can)								
Celery Salt (Box)								
Kosher Salt (Box)								
Cola Syrup (Gal)								
Ginger Ale Syrup (Gal)								
Lemon Lime Syrup (Gal)								
Quinine Syrup (Gal)								

PAPER GOODS

4	Short Straws (Box)	1/3	2/2	1/3	2/2				
4	Long Straws (Box)	2/2	2/2	1/3	3/				
2	Stir Sticks (Box)	2/0	1/1	2/0	1/1				
2	Cocktail Picks (Box)	0/2	1/1	1/1	1/1				
2	Umbrellas (Box)	2/0	2/0	1/1	2/0				

FIGURE 6

BAR SUPPLY PURCHASING SHEET (Cont.)

MONTH:
DAY:

GLASSWARE (Cases)										
4	High Ball Glass #2338	4 / 0	4 / 0	3 / 1	4 / 0					
2	Tall Hi Ball Glass #1616	2 / 0	1 / 1	1 / 1	2 / 0					
2	Rock Glass #1613	2 / 0	0 / 2	2 / 0	2 / 0					
2	Bucket Glass #1615	2 / 0	2 / 0	2 / 0	2 / 0					
2	Martini Glass #3601	2 / 0	2 / 0	2 / 0	2 / 0					
2	Cocktail Glass #8461	2 / 0	2 / 0	2 / 0	2 / 0					
1	Sour Glass #8075	1 / 0	0 / 1	1 / 0	1 / 0					
1	Margarita Glass #8415	1 / 0	1 / 0	1 / 0	1 / 0					
4	Wine Glass #8360	3 / 1	3 / 1	4 / 0	4 / 0					
1	Champagne Glass #8077	1 / 0	1 / 0	1 / 0	1 / 0					
1	Brandy Snifter #3704	1 / 0	1 / 0	1 / 0	1 / 0					
1	Cordial Glass #8491	1 / 0	1 / 0	1 / 0	1 / 0					
1	Shot Glass #48	1 / 0	1 / 0	1 / 0	1 / 0					
1	Beer Mug #5205	1 / 0	1 / 0	1 / 0	1 / 0					
2	Half Liter #789	2 / 0	1 / 1	2 / 0	1 / 1					
2	Full Liter #795	2 / 0	1 / 1	2 / 0	2 / 0					
MISCELLANEOUS SUPPLIES										
2	BAR SPOON	2 / 0	2 / 0	2 / 0	2 / 0					
2	MIXING CAN STRAINER	2 / 0	2 / 0	1 / 1	2 / 0					
2	MIXING GLASS STRAINER	2 / 0	2 / 0	1 / 1	2 / 0					

FOOD REQUISITION SHEET

Week of: ___10/2___

	M	T	W	Th	F	S	SU	TOTAL	UNIT COST	EXTENSION
FRUIT										
Bananas (ea)	6	Ø	Ø	6	12	Ø	Ø	24	.11	2.64
Celery (head)	1	Ø	1	Ø	1	1	1	5	.38	1.90
Lemons (ea)	2	2	3	2	6	4	2	21	.18	3.78
Limes (ea)	10	10	12	12	24	18	12	88	.12	10.56
Oranges (ea)	2	2	2	3	6	6	4	25	.09	2.25
Pineapples (ea)	Ø	Ø	1	Ø	2	1	Ø	4	1.00	4.00
Strawberries (can)	Ø	1	Ø	Ø	1	Ø	Ø	2	4.12	8.24
DAIRY										
Cream (qt)	1	Ø	1	1	2	2	1	8	.71	5.68
Whipped Cream (can)	Ø	1	2	2	3	2	1	11	.82	20.02
JUICES										
Grapefruit (can)	1	0	0	0	1	0	0	2	1.24	2.48
Orange (½ gal)	1	2	2	1	3	2	2	13	1.10	14.30
Pineapple (can)	1	0	0	1	1	0	0	3	1.14	3.41
Tomato (can)	2	0	2	2	6	4	4	20	.91	18.20
MISCELLANEOUS										
Tabasco (btl)	0	0	0	0	1	0	1	2	.31	.62
Sugar (cup)	1	0	0	0	1	0	0	2	.22	.44
Worcestershire (btl)	0	0	0	0	1	0	2	3	.42	1.26
BARTENDERS INITIALS:										

TOTAL COST OF REQUISITIONED FOOD: 99.79

FIGURE 7

through a Build To process, using separate ordering sheets for each distributor.

Restaurant bars can simplify this process by simply requisitioning the food items on a daily basis from the kitchen inventory. For control purposes, a requisition sheet should be used. Each morning, the day bartender should note all of the food items taken from the kitchen on the food requisition sheet. At the end of each week the manager can total the cost of those items and charge that total to bar supplies, instead of the kitchen.

For the week illustrated in Figure 7, the $99.79 in food items requisitioned from the kitchen would be charged to bar supplies.

Chapter 2

INVENTORY CONTROLS

One of the most important aspects of professional bar management is inventory control. Because bar management involves the organization and storage of several hundred bottles of liquor, beer, and wine, it's imperative to establish controls that will allow the manager to maintain a keen awareness of the entire inventory. Such controls are designed to diminish both theft and the confusion caused by unorganized and misplaced inventory.

Ideally, the entire liquor inventory (liquor, beer, and wine) should be stored in only two places—the liquor storeroom and the bar itself. Unfortunately, most bars are built with only a limited amount of refrigeration and, as a result, either a portion of the kitchen walk-in cooler or, preferably, a separate locked refrigeration unit has to be used as the third storage area.

THE LIQUOR STOREROOM
Inventory Organization

As the diagram in Figure 8 illustrates, the liquor storeroom should be divided into areas, each designated to stock a particular type of liquor (gins, rums, vodkas, etc.). Each of these general areas should then be subdivided and labeled, so that *each item has a specifically marked storage area.* Every item stored in the liquor storeroom, from swizzle sticks to champagne, should have a specified storage area. As the old saying goes, "A place for everything and everything in its place."

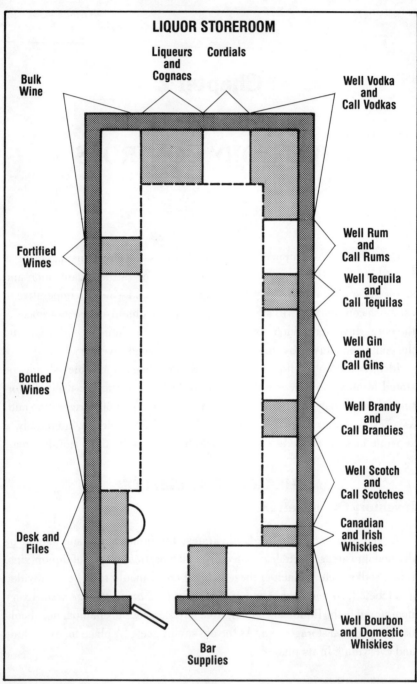

FIGURE 8

Construction

Normally, the larger the storeroom the better, for two reasons. First, it gives the manager the added storage space needed when purchasing liquor in large quantities, and secondly, it's far easier to properly organize the inventory within a larger area.

The room will usually be used for the storage of bottled wines as well as liquor and should therefore be well ventilated. Because bottled wines have to be stored on their sides, it's very desirable to furnish the storeroom with wine racks. If there are no racks, the wines will have to be stored in their cases, which will tend to occupy a considerable amount of space.

The room should be constructed with deep shelving from the floor to the ceiling lining each wall. Each shelf should be at least three feet deep, and there should be at least 18 inches between shelves.

The storeroom is often the best place to keep a desk and file cabinet for the storage of such items as employee files, inventory control forms, current discount sheets, sales records, invoices, and statements. The center of the room should remain empty so that it will be available to be used for a temporary storage area for new deliveries.

Storeroom Inventory Control

Besides equipping the storeroom door with a dead bolt lock, a manager can greatly add to the security of the liquor storeroom through the use of a perpetual inventory system. Such a system involves first recording the actual bottle count of each item stored in the storeroom, and then carefully logging inventory changes (deliveries or inventory transferred to the bar) on a daily basis. As a result, the manager will have a record of the actual storeroom inventory at all times and will be able to verify these records in minutes through an actual bottle count.

Through the use of this system, the theft or misplacing of any inventory can be quickly spotted, but only if the manager maintains consistent records. A perpetual inventory system is only as reliable as the degree of consistency in which it is maintained. Therefore, a manager must make it a habit to set aside ten minutes each day to bring the system up to date. Each time an item is removed or added to the inventory, the transaction should be recorded and verified through an actual count of remaining bottles of that item. This entire process should be handled only by the manager and the records should be kept under lock.

Most methods of operating a perpetual inventory system are simply variations of either the card file system or the more convenient sheet system.

The Card File: Perpetual Inventory System

A manager can easily construct a perpetual inventory system using only lined file cards and a file box. Each card should be designed similar to the one illustrated in Figure 9.

On 10/1, the bar requisitioned two quarts of Jack Daniels from the storeroom, leaving ten quarts in the storeroom. On 10/2, one more quart was requisitioned and two cases (24 quarts) were delivered, leaving 33 quarts in the storeroom at the end of the day. No inventory changes occurred on 10/3.

INVENTORY FILE CARD

Jack Daniel's (Quarts)											
Date	OI	Rq	NI	DEL	FI	Date	OI	Rq	NI	DEL	FI
10/1	12	2	10	—	10						
10/2	10	1	9	24	33						
10/4	33	2	31	—	31						
	31										

Date = The date the inventory adjustment occurred

OI = The opening storeroom inventory

Rq = Requisitioned inventory

NI = The new inventory

DEL = Deliveries on that day

FI = The final storeroom inventory

FIGURE 9

The Sheet: Perpetual Inventory System

A very efficient means of maintaining a perpetual inventory system is through the use of a perpetual inventory sheet and a clipboard. A portion of such a sheet is illustrated in Figure 10.

LIQUOR PERPETUAL INVENTORY SHEET

American Whiskey	M	T	W	Th	F		
	1/2	1/2	1/3	1/4	1/5	1/6	
Early Times	2 / 8			1 / 7			
I. W. Harper	1 / 4	+6 / 10					
Jack Daniel's							

FIGURE 10

Each box on the sheet represents a day. The top number is the number of bottles removed from the storeroom and the bottom number represents the number of bottles remaining. In Figure 10, on Monday, January 1, two bottles of Early Times were requisitioned from the storeroom by the bar, and eight bottles remained in the storeroom. No more Early Times was requisitioned until Thursday, January 4, when one more bottle was removed, leaving seven. On Tuesday, January 2, there was a delivery of six quarts of I. W. Harper, bringing the total inventory to ten quarts.

A perpetual inventory sheet actually consists of about five or six sheets, the last of which is used to record deliveries, as noted in Figure 11.

INVENTORY SHEET-DELIVERIES

Date	Distributor	Items Purchased	Total Cost
10/17	YOUNG'S	1. CS. Lt. CUTTY SARK (910) 2. CS. Lt. BEEFEATER (947)	222.84

FIGURE 11

On 10/17 there was a delivery from Young's, which consisted of one case of Cutty Sark and two cases of Beefeater, both of which were liters. The bottle prices are in parentheses.

An example of a full perpetual inventory sheet is illustrated in Figure 12. The purchase sheet would be attached at the end.

THE BAR

Inventory Organization

For efficiency and inventory control purposes, there must be an adequate backup supply of all liquors, beers, and wines kept at the bar itself. The actual number of bottles should depend on the daily rate of usage. If at all possible, added inventory should never have to be obtained from the storeroom during the middle of a shift. Once the bar is stocked in the morning, the liquor storeroom should be locked and opened only for deliveries.

This backup inventory can amount to quite a large number of bottles, especially in the busier bars. As a result, management has to take steps to see that this inventory is well controlled and each bottle always remains accounted for.

This is best done through implementing a "par" system. Management determines exactly how many bottles of each item will need to be stored at the bar; that number is referred to as that item's par. For example, if it's determined that three bottles of Chivas Regal should be kept at the bar at all times, the par for Chivas Regal would be three. One bottle would remain open and kept in the display case, and two bottles would remain sealed and kept in the storage cabinet.

Every item in the entire liquor, beer, and wine inventory should be assigned a par. By doing this, management can be guaranteed that the bottle inventory kept at the bar will always be the same. Every morning, when the emptied bottles are replaced with new bottles, the entire bar should be at par.

The specific storage areas should be organized as follows:

The Storage Cabinets

Because of the large number of brands involved, and because the pars will vary, a par sheet similar to the one in Figure 13 should be posted inside each storage cabinet door and each refrigerator door. It should reflect the exact inventory stored within that area.

The sample par sheet was taken from a large storage area in a single station bar. As was explained earlier, a par of three would indicate that there should

LIQUOR PERPETUAL INVENTORY SHEET

	M	T	W	Th	F	S	SU	M	T	W	Th	F	S	SU	
DAY: DATE:															TOTAL SALES

WELL LIQUOR

VODKA															
BOURBON															
GIN															
SCOTCH															
RUM															
BRANDY															
TEQUILA															

AMERICAN WHISKEY

EARLY TIMES															
I.W. HARPER															
Jack Daniel's															
Jim Beam															
Old Grand Dad															
Old Overholt															
Old Taylor															
Seagram's 7 Crown															
Wild Turkey															

CANADIAN WHISKY

Canadian Club															
Crown Royal															
Seagram's V.O.															

SCOTCH WHISKY

Ballantine's															
Black & White															
Chivas Regal															
Cutty Sark															
Dewar's															
J & B															
Black Label															
Red Label															

IRISH WHISKEY

Murphey's															
Old Bushmills															

FIGURE 12

LIQUOR PERPETUAL INVENTORY SHEET (Cont.)

DAY:	M	T	W	Th	F	S	SU	M	T	W	Th	F	S	SU	TOTAL
DATE:															SALES

GIN

Beefeater															
Bombay															
Tanqueray															

VODKA

Smirnoff															
Stolichnaya															

TEQUILA

Jose Cuervo Gold															
Jose Cuervo 1800															

RUM

Bacardi Silver															
Bacardi Amber															
Bacardi 151															
Myer's Rum															

BRANDY—COGNAC

Christian Bros.															
Courvoisier															
Hennessy															
Remy Martin															

SWEET WINES—VERMOUTH

S. Vermouth															
D. Vermouth															
Dry Sack															
Dubonnet															
Harvey's															
Ruby Port															

CORDIALS

Anisette															
Blackberry Brandy															

LIQUOR PERPETUAL INVENTORY SHEET (Cont.)

CORDIALS (Cont.)

Cacao—Dark	
Cacao—White	
Cherry Brandy	
Creme de Banana	
Creme de Cassis	
Creme de Noyaux	
Menthe—Green	
Menthe—White	
Peppermint Schnps	
Sloe Gin	
Triple Sec	

LIQUEURS

Amaretto	
Benedictine	
Drambuie	
Galliano	
Grand Marnier	
Kahlua	
Metaxa	
Tuaca	
Strega	

BULK WINE

BURGUNDY	
ROSE	
CHABLIS	

BOTTLED WINES

RED:	
Cab. Sauvignon	
Mouton Cadet	
Pinot Noir (Full)	
Pinot Noir (Half)	
ROSE:	
Gamay Rose	
Mateus (Full)	
Mateus (Half)	
WHITE:	
Chenin Blanc	
Riesling	
Pinot Chardonnay	

PAR LEVELS

WELL BOURBON	9	Jose Cuervo Gold	3
WELL VODKA	9	Jose Cuervo 1980	3
WELL GIN	9		
WELL SCOTCH	9	Bacardi Silver	3
WELL RUM	6	Bacardi Amber	3
WELL TEQUILA	6	Bacardi 151	3
WELL BRANDY	6	Myer's	3

Early Times	3	Christian Brothers	3
I. W. Harper	3		
Jack Daniel's	3	Sweet Vermouth	3
Jim Beam	3	Dry Vermouth	3
Old Grand Dad	3	Dry Sack	3
Old Overholt	3	Harvey's Bristol Cream	3
Old Taylor	3	Ruby Port	3
7 Crown	3		
Wild Turkey	3	Amaretto	3
		B&B	3
Canadian Club	3	Drambuie	3
Crown Royal	3	Galliano	3
V.O.	3	Kahlua	3
		Metaxa	3
Murphy's	3	Tuaca	3
Old Bushmills	3		
		Anisette	3
Beefeaters	3	Blackberry Brandy	3
Bombay	3	Cherry Brandy	3
Tanqueray	3	Creme de Banana	3
		Creme de Cacao (Dark)	3
Ballantines	3	Creme de Cacao (Light)	3
Black & White	3	Creme de Cassis	3
Chivas Regal	3	Creme de Menthe	
Cutty Sark	3	(Green)	3
Dewar's	3	Creme de Menthe	
J&B	3	(White)	3
Black Label	3	Creme de Noyaux	3
Red Label	3	Peppermint Schnapps	3
		Sloe Gin	3
Smirnoff	3	Triple Sec	3

FIGURE 13

be two full bottles in the storage cabinet and one open bottle located in either the display cabinet or well area.

The Well Area

The well area should be organized in a set manner and maintained in that manner at all times. Even though bartenders may comment that they prefer to organize the bottles in an arrangement they're more comfortable with, this should not be allowed. Generally, the more "rearranging" bartenders do, the more unorganized the bar tends to become. Management should always demand consistency in inventory organization.

To guarantee consistency in this area, a diagram of the well setup should be posted inside the door of the main storage cabinet, across from the par sheet.

As the diagram in Figure 14 illustrates, even the speed racks should be organized in a set manner.

The Display Case

The display case is another area that should always be organized in a set manner. To ensure this, the manager should tape the name of each brand of liquor to the specific spot in the display case on which that bottle of liquor should stand. Then, when returning bottles to the display case, the bartender need only remember to place each bottle directly on top of the tape bearing its name.

After this system is implemented, bartenders should never have an excuse for the display case being less than perfectly organized.

The Bar Inventory Control

Inventory at the bar is controlled simply by maintaining and continually checking the par system. Each morning the manager should replace the bottles emptied the day before with new bottles from the storeroom, and then check the entire bar inventory to verify that every item is at par.

The sales of the various bottled beers and wines can be determined through counting the remaining inventories. For example, if the par for Budweiser beer is 24 and there are only ten remaining, it would be deter-

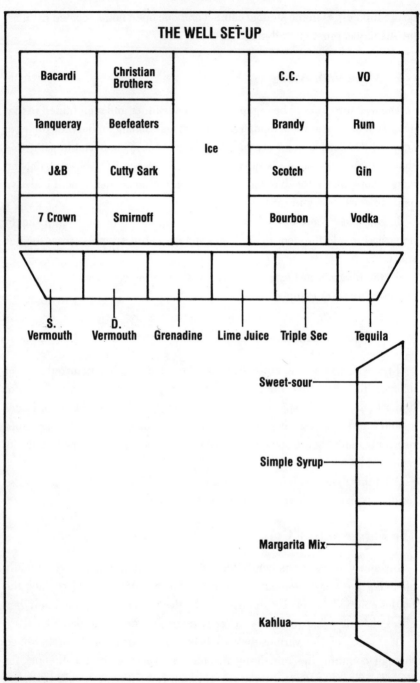

FIGURE 14

mined that 14 were sold and so 14 would be brought to the bar to bring Budweiser back up to par. The same logic should be used for bottled wines. If the par for full bottles of Mateus is eight and only five remain, it would be determined that three were sold and, therefore, three would be brought to the bar to bring full bottles of Mateus back up to par.

Before opening the bar, the manager should carefully check that each brand of liquor, beer, and wine is at par. To simplify this process the backup inventory should be stored in a very organized manner. In the par sheet in Figure 13 all the call liquors had a par of three, and the well liquors had a par of either nine or six. Standardizing the par levels makes it easier for them to be checked. If the manager were to establish the levels solely on the basis of usage he might have created nine different levels of par, which would have been difficult to check and therefore would have eventually led to mistakes.

This daily stocking of the bar obviously will not in itself control the liquor cost. After all, simply because three full bottles of Mateus happen to be missing does not necessarily mean that they were sold. One or even all of them may have been stolen or simply given away by the bartender. The same reasoning holds true for emptied bottles of liquor. An empty bottle is no guarantee that all of the contents were sold. It's very possible that a good portion of that bottle may have been served without charge or may have even been drunk by the bartender.

These are all possibilities, and they will be examined in detail in Chapter 3, on cost analysis. Before a manager can realistically analyze costs he or she must first control inventory through keeping exact daily records of the inventory turnover. Each day, all of the emptied bottles of beer and wine should be recorded on a daily requisition sheet. Figure 15 shows an example of such a sheet. The term "requisition" refers to the new inventory being requisitioned from the storeroom by the bar.

The well liquors, house wines, and all of the beers are printed on the sample daily requisition sheet, while the blank spaces are used to write in the call liquors, liqueurs, and bottled wines.

If additional inventory has to be obtained from the storeroom during the middle of a shift, the added inventory should immediately be noted on the requisition sheet. For example, if the bartender sold out of bottled Michelob and an extra case (24 bottles) was brought to the bar, the bartender should immediately write +24 on that day's requisition sheet. Then, at the end of the shift, if there were only four bottles of Michelob remaining, and the par

DAILY REQUISITION SHEET

DAY: _____   DATE: _____

	Total	Cost	Extension		Total	Cost	Extension
Well Liquors				Bottled Beers:			
Vodka				Budweiser			
Bourbon				Michelob			
Gin				Lite			
Scotch				Heineken			
Rum				Draft Beer:			
Brandy				Millers			
Tequila				House Wines:			
Call liquors, liqueurs and				Burgundy			
aperitif wines:				Chablis			
				Rose			
				Bottled Wines:			

TOTAL COST OF ENTIRE REQUISITIONED INVENTORY:

FIGURE 15

DAILY REQUISITION SHEET IN USE

The following inventory used:

6	Well Vodka	28	Budweiser	2	Half bottles of Pinot Noir
4	Well Bourbon	19	Michelob	1	Full bottle of Petite Sirah
2	Well Gin	21	Lite	3	Half bottles of Blue Nun
3	Well Scotch	10	Heineken	1	Full bottle of Blue Nun
1	Well Rum	1	Keg of Millers	1	Full bottle of Riesling
2	V.O.			1	Half bottle of Mumm's Champagne
1	Early Times	1	Gallon of Burgundy		
1	Beefeaters	3	Gallons of Chablis		
1	Cutty Sark	2	Gallons of Rose		
2	J&B				
1	Kahlua				
1	Galliano				
1	Dry Sack				
1	Dubonnet				

Would be listed as follows:

DAILY REQUISITION SHEET

DAY: _MONDAY_   DATE: _10/15_

	Total	Cost	Extension		Total	Cost	Extension
Well Liquors				**Bottled Beers:**			
Vodka	6			Budweiser	28		
Bourbon	4			Michelob	19		
Gin	2			Lite	21		
Scotch	3			Heineken	10		
Rum	1			**Draft Beer:**			
Brandy	Ø			Millers	1		
Tequila	Ø			**House Wines:**			
Call liquors, liqueurs and				Burgundy	1		
aperitif wines:				Chablis	3		
V.O.	2			Rose	2		
EARLY TIMES	1			**Bottled Wines:**			
BEEFEATERS	1			½ PINOT NOIR	2		
CUTTY SARK	1			PETITE SIRAH	1		
JB	2			½ BLUE NUN	3		
KAHLUA	1			BLUE NUN	1		
GALLIANO	1			RIESLING	1		
DRY SACK	1			½ MUMM'S	1		
DUBONNET	1						

FIGURE 16

for Michelob was 24, the bartender would remember to record the usage as 44 (20 + 24) instead of simply 20.

SECONDARY STORAGE AREAS

If the refrigeration space at the bar is limited and a remote refrigeration unit has to be utilized, this separate area should be considered as part of the bar and, all items stored in this area should also be assigned a par.

Each morning the actual bar inventory should be brought to par with inventory taken from the secondary storage area, then the secondary storage area should be brought to par with inventory taken from the storeroom.

The same policy should hold true in the event that the liquor room is small and a secondary dry storage area is utilized. Only the inventory stored in the main liquor storeroom should be controlled through the use of a perpetual inventory system; all the other storage areas should be thought of as being part of the bar and, therefore, controlled through par systems.

TRANSFERRING INVENTORY

The simple tasks of stocking the bar and storing deliveries can lead to surprising confusion and mistakes if the manager fails to establish and rigidly enforce firm rules, rules similar to those listed below.

Stocking the Bar

The closing bartender should count all of the emptied bottles of liquor and the remaining bottles of beer and wine, and then record all of the used inventory on the Daily Requisition Sheet.

The closing manager should first verify the numbers on the requisition sheet through an actual bottle count. Then, he or she should transfer all of the emptied bottles to the liquor storeroom, and clip the requisition sheet to the appropriate clipboard in the storeroom.

The opening manager will exchange the emptied bottles for full bottles and recheck to see that all of the bottles have been properly recorded on the requisition sheet. After stocking the entire bar he or she'll check every item to see that it is indeed at its proper level of par.

Finally, all of the storeroom inventory adjustments should immediately be

THE LIQUOR PRICE SHEET

The first row of boxes indicates the opening prices of each item. The following rows are used to indicate price changes. Of the items listed, only the prices of Well Bourbon and Beefeaters have changed in this example.

LIQUOR PRICE SHEET

DOMESTIC WHISKEY				GIN				
BOURBON	4.26 4.45	4.60		GIN	3.54			
Early Times	6.20			Beefeaters	9.26	9.45		
I. W. Harper	6.90			Bombay	8.75			
Jack Daniels	9.00			Tanqueray	9.25			

FIGURE 17

noted on the perpetual inventory sheet and verified through an actual bottle count of the remaining inventories of the adjusted items.

This entire "double checking" process takes only a few extra minutes but can virtually guarantee the elimination of both error and unrecognized theft.

RECEIVING DELIVERIES

The following rules should always be followed when receiving a delivery of liquor.

1) Deliveries should only be received by management.

2) The *sizes, brands* and *quantities* of all items should be verified *before* signing the invoice.

3) The delivery should *immediately* be transferred into the locked liquor storeroom.

4) On the day of the delivery, the cases should be opened and the bottles stored in their assigned areas of the storeroom. They should be arranged in an orderly fashion, with their labels facing outward.

5) The added inventory should immediately be noted on the perpetual inventory sheet.

6) Any price variations should be noted on the price sheet.

7) The total cost of the delivery should be noted on the monthly record sheet and the invoice should be properly filed.

To avoid mistakes, this entire process should always take place on the day of the delivery.

The liquor price sheet mentioned in step six is designed to enable the manager to be aware of price changes. The manner in which this sheet is used is illustrated in Figure 17.

Chapter 3

SALES COSTS

By implementing sound purchasing policies, effective inventory controls, and the detailed employee training programs discussed in later chapters, a manager should bring sales costs to a very desirable level. To maintain those costs at such a level a manager will have to be knowledgeable enough to conduct regular physical inventories, calculate actual costs, analyze and correctly interpret those costs, and implement cost control techniques.

This chapter will deal with these subjects, dividing them into the areas of calculating costs, cost analysis, and cost controls.

CALCULATING ACTUAL COSTS

Record Keeping

Accurate record keeping can be considered the first phase in the study of sales costs. The various costs cannot even be calculated, much less correctly analyzed, if itemized sales and purchasing records are not accurately maintained.

Sales Records

It is best to record both the total net sales of the day and the itemized sales of liquor, beer, and wine. Obtaining these figures is easily done through

WEEK'S LIQUOR SALES RECORD

DATE	LIQUOR	WINE	BEER	DAILY	TOTAL
10/2	585 10	110 70	53 40	749 20	749 20
10/3	609 90	161 50	80 30	851 70	1600 90
10/4	685 55	170 55	67 40	923 50	2524 40
10/5	748 30	118 40	74 70	941 40	3465 80
10/6	1791 20	309 10	96 90	2197 20	5663 00
10/7	1242 70	279 45	85 95	1608 10	7271 10
10/8	397 10	71 40	36 10	504 60	7775 70
	6059 95	1221 10	494 75	———	7775 70

FIGURE 18

establishing separate service keys on the bar cash register for each of the categories of alcoholic beverages. The bartender need only ring the sales price of each item served on the appropriate key to supply the manager with itemized sales readings.

Besides giving the manager the opportunity to follow the various sales trends within each category, this policy will also give the manager the opportunity to calculate the percentage cost for each category, as will be explained later in the chapter. Figure 18 is an example of how the daily liquor sales might be recorded for one week.

Purchasing Records

Itemized purchasing records should also be maintained, as illustrated in Figure 19. For cost analysis purposes, the bar supplies will have to be broken down into food and non-food items. The cost of the food items purchased (cherries, mixes, etc.) should be recorded under the "Food" heading, and will later be added to the cost of the food items requisitioned from the kitchen to determine the total value of the non-alcoholic food items sold in the bar. The cost of all of the other bar supplies purchased should be recorded under the appropriate heading.

To simplify bookkeeping, restaurants usually prefer to simply record the non-food items used in the bar together with similar items used in the kitchen and dining room (glassware, laundry, paper goods, etc.). This might be an

BAR PURCHASES

DATE	LIQUOR	BEER	WINE	FOOD	GLASSWARE	PAPER GOODS	MISC. SUPPLIES	EQUIPMENT	LAUNDRY	CLEANING SUPPLIES
9/1		71.40							11.40	
9/2	2,484.71		412.09							11.32
9/3	712.80			73.50	41.70	11.15	17.10			
9/4										
9/5										
9/6										
9/7										
	3,197.51	71.40	412.09	73.50	41.70	11.15	17.10	0	11.40	11.32
9/8		109.10							9.50	
9/9										
9/10				54.81		41.93		115.71		
9/11										
9/12										
9/13										
9/14										
	3,197.51	180.50	412.09	128.31	41.70	53.08	17.10	115.71	20.90	11.32
9/15		85.10							13.10	9.27
9/16										
9/17				48.73	62.94	47.54	4.08			
9/18										
9/19										
9/20										
9/21										
	3,197.51	265.60	412.09	177.04	104.64	100.62	21.18	115.71	34.00	20.59
9/22		115.40							12.60	
9/23										
9/24										

FIGURE 19

acceptable policy for smaller establishments, but it is much better policy for management to maximize controls through detailed purchasing records.

Conducting a Physical Inventory

Before actual cost can be determined, an exact physical inventory will have to be taken of every alcoholic beverage and food item either purchased or requisitioned for the bar. Accuracy is imperative in the counting of each item, because the figures obtained through taking the physical inventory will eventually determine the accuracy of the cost figures.

The physical inventory should be taken after the bar has been stocked and all items are at par. An example of a physical inventory sheet is given in Figure 20.

In the sample sheet, the "par" column refers to the number of sealed bottles in storage at the bar. Because the bar should be fully stocked at the time the inventory is taken, these figures should be known before the actual counting begins.

The "bar" column refers to the opened bottles. Each bottle should be estimated to the nearest tenth. In a multiple station bar there may be a number of opened bottles of each brand. In such an instance, the volume of each bottle will be estimated and the combined total of all of the bottles will be recorded in the "bar" column.

The remaining inventory of each item should be located in the storeroom and should be recorded under the "S.R." heading.

The figures listed under the "total" heading should represent the combined total of the figures listed in the first three columns, while the "cost" column should list the unit cost of each item. The unit cost should be taken from the price sheet, but in transferring the prices the manager should be careful that the price is for the correct size. If some items happen to be stocked in two sizes, one of the sizes should be recorded in the "other liquor inventory" section.

The "extension" heading simply refers to the actual cash value of the inventory of each item, and can be determined by multiplying the "cost" figure by the "total" figure.

A segment of a completed physical inventory would look like Figure 21.

After the physical inventory has been completed and extended, the totals should be itemized into three categories, *liquor, beer,* and *wine.* Only the

LIQUOR PHYSICAL INVENTORY

DATE: _____

LIQUOR: _____

BEER: _____

WINE: _____

FOOD SUPPLIES: _____

TOTAL INVENTORY:

DOMESTIC WHISKEY

	PAR	BAR	S.R.	TOTAL	COST	EXTENSION
BOURBON						
Early Times						
I. W. Harper						
Jack Daniel's						
Jim Beam						
Old Grand Dad						
Old Overholt						
Old Taylor						
Seagram's 7 Crown						
Wild Turkey						

CANADIAN WHISKY

Canadian Club						
Crown Royal						
Seagram's V.O.						

SCOTCH WHISKY

SCOTCH						
Black & White						
Chivas Regal						
Cutty Sark						
Dewar's						
J & B						
Black Label						
Red Label						

FIGURE 20

LIQUOR PHYSICAL INVENTORY (Cont.)

IRISH WHISKEY	PAR	BAR	S.R.	TOTAL	COST	EXTENSION
Murphey's						
Old Bushmills						

GIN

GIN						
Beefeater						
Bombay						
Tanqueray						

VODKA

VODKA						
Smirnoff						
Stolichnaya						

TEQUILA

TEQUILA						
Jose Cuervo Gold						
Jose Cuervo 1800						

RUM

RUM						
Bacardi Silver						
Bacardi Amber						
Bacardi 151						
Myer's						

BRANDY—COGNAC

BRANDY						
Christian Bros.						
Courvoisier						
Hennessy						
Remy Martin						

LIQUOR PHYSICAL INVENTORY (Cont.)

SWEET WINES—VERMOUTH

	PAR	BAR	S.R.	TOTAL	COST	EXTENSION
S. Vermouth						
D. Vermouth						
Dry Sack						
Dubonnet						
Harvey's						
Ruby Port						

CORDIALS

Anisette						
Blackberry Brandy						
Cacao—Dark						
Cacao—White						
Cherry Brandy						
Creme de Banana						
Creme de Cassis						
Creme de Noyaux						
Menthe—Green						
Menthe—White						
Peppermint Schnps.						
Sloe Gin						
Triple Sec						

LIQUEURS

Amaretto						
Benedictine						
Drambuie						
Galliano						
Grand Marnier						
Kahlua						
Metaxa						
Tuaca						
Strega						

LIQUOR PHYSICAL INVENTORY (Cont.)

OTHER LIQUOR INVENTORY

	PAR	BAR	S.R.	TOTAL	COST	EXTENSION

BEER

	PAR	BAR	S.R.	TOTAL	COST	EXTENSION
Budweiser						
Coors						
Michelob						
Light						
Millers (½ Keg)						

BULK WINES

	PAR	BAR	S.R.	TOTAL	COST	EXTENSION
BURGUNDY						
ROSE						
CHABLIS						

BOTTLED WINES

RED WINES:	PAR	BAR	S.R.	TOTAL	COST	EXTENSION
Cabernet Sauvignon						
Mouton Cadet						
Pinot Noir (Full)						
Pinot Noir (Half)						

ROSE WINES:						
Gamay Rose						
Mateus (Full)						
Mateus (Half)						

LIQUOR PHYSICAL INVENTORY (Cont.)

BOTTLED WINES (Cont.)

	PAR	BAR	S.R.	TOTAL	COST	EXTENSION
WHITE WINES:						
Chenin Blanc						
Liebfraumilch (Full)						
Liebfraumilch (Half)						
Pinot Chardonnay						

CHAMPAGNE

Jacques Bonet						
Mumm's (Full)						
Mumm's (Half)						

FOOD SUPPLIES:

Red Cherries						
Green Cherries						
Olives						
Onions						
Grenadine						
Lime Juice						
Sweet Sour Mix						
Margarita Mix						
Mai Tai Mix						
Pina Colada Mix						
Bloody Mary Mix						
Orange Flower Water						
Celery Salt						
Kosher Salt						
Bitters						
Boullion						
Nutmeg						
Quinine Syrup						
Cola Syrup						
Seven Up Syrup						

CANADIAN WHISKY

	PAR	BAR	S.R.	TOTAL	COST	EXTENSION
Canadian Club	2	.7	13	15.7	7.87	123.55
Crown Royal	2	.3	9	11.3	12.48	141.02
Seagram's V.O.	2	.9	21	23.9	7.92	189.28

FIGURE 21

value of the house wines and the bottled wines should be listed under the wine heading, while the fortified wines (sherry, vermouths, port, etc.) should be listed under the liquor heading.

Calculating Percentage Costs

The seller's costs are usually referred to and analyzed in terms of their relative percentage to total net sales, which is why costs are usually referred to as *percentage costs* or simply P.C. For example, if a bar used an average of twenty dollars' worth of liquor for every hundred dollars' worth of sales, the liquor P.C. would be twenty percent.

Calculating the percentage cost is easily done through taking a physical inventory at the beginning and again at the end of an established length of time, by keeping accurate sales and purchasing records throughout that time, and by using the following two formulas:

$$P.C. = \frac{\text{Inventory Loss}}{\text{Total Net Sales}}$$

Inventory Loss = (Opening Inventory + Purchases) − Closing Inventory

The term "inventory loss" refers to the actual dollar cost of the inventory that was used.

An example of exactly how these formulas are used is given below. In the example the percentage cost of alcoholic beverages within the month of November is being calculated. The first inventory was taken on November first, before the bar opened, and the second inventory was taken on December first, again before the bar opened. Notice that the entire calculation is only a two step process: first the inventory loss is determined, and then the actual percentage cost is derived.

Calculating percentage cost:

Opening inventory (November 1): $5,345.79
Closing inventory (December 1): $5,793.47
Total November net sales: $24,795.43
Total November purchases (liquor, beer, and wine): $5,814.52

Inventory Loss = (Opening Inventory + Purchases) − Closing Inventory
= (5,345.79 + 5,814.52) − 5,793.47
= $5,366.84

$$P.C. = \frac{\text{Inventory Loss}}{\text{Net Sales}} = \frac{5,366.84}{24,795.43} = .2164$$

November P.C. = 21.64%

Calculating Itemized Percentage Costs

When analyzing a bar operation, the term "percentage cost" is very relative to the area of concern—percentage costs of liquor, beer, and wine may vary. In the example above of the calculation of the November P.C., the 21.64 percent represented the *combined* costs of all alcoholic beverages divided by the total net bar sales for the month. This figure is sometimes referred to as the *pouring cost*.

Determining the itemized costs, specifically the percentage cost of liquor, beer, wine, and food supplies, is also very important. These figures can be calculated using the same two step process that was used to derive the pouring cost. All that will be needed are itemized sales records, purchasing records, and physical inventories.

Below is a detailed example of the step by step procedures for calculating the individual percentage costs for liquor, beer, wine and non-alcoholic food supplies. Because the food items are sold as mixes and garnishes for drinks, rather than separately, the percentage cost of those items is based on total sales instead of itemized sales as in the case of liquor, beer, and wine.

Calculating itemized percentage costs (one month's records):

Total Net Sales:	$27,240.20
Liquor	19,587.10
Beer	2,411.00
Wine	5,242.10

Total Purchases:	6,227.84
Liquor	3,548.71
Beer	521.50
Wine	1,625.83
Food	531.80
Opening Inventory:	6,540.72
Liquor	5,241.50
Beer	308.90
Wine	850.10
Food	140.52
Closing Inventory:	6,863.39
Liquor	5,578.40
Beer	250.10
Wine	910.78
Food	124.11

Calculating each percentage cost:

Liquor P.C.:
1) $(5,241.50 + 3,548.71) - 5,578.39 = 3,211.81$
2) $(3,211.81 / 19,587.9) = .1640$ or <u>16.40%</u>

Beer P.C.:
1) $(308.90 + 521.50) - 210.10 = 620.30$
2) $(620.30 / 2,411.00) = .2573$ or <u>25.73%</u>

Wine P.C.:
1) $(850.10 + 1,625.83) - 910.78 = 1,565.15$
2) $(1,565.15 / 5,242.10) = .2986$ or <u>29.86%</u>

Food Supplies P.C.:
1) $(140.52 + 531.80) - 124.11 = 548.21$
2) $(548.21 / 27,240.20) = .0201$ or <u>2.01%</u>

Figure 22 shows a cost breakdown sheet, which should supply the manager with all the information needed pertaining to actual costs. These sheets should be filled in each month and kept on file with the physical inventory sheets.

MONTHLY COST BREAKDOWN

MONTH: __MAY__

	SALES	%	COST	%
LIQUOR	19,587 10	71.91	3,211 81	16.39
BEER	2,411 00	8.85	620 30	25.72
WINE	5,242 10	19.24	1,565 15	29.85

POURING COST	27,240 20		5,397 26	19.81
FOOD SUPPLIES	27,240 20		548 21	2.01
TOTAL COST	27,240 20		5,937 47	21.82

FIGURE 22

COST ANALYSIS

Once itemized bar costs are derived, the next step is a detailed analysis of each cost. The actual costs are not always what they should be, and when they are not, the bar manager must be able to realize it.

Beer Cost

Analyzing the beer cost is an easy task, because calculating what the beer cost should have been is relatively simple. The only information that will be needed is the sales price, unit cost, and the number of units sold of each brand of beer. If a perpetual inventory system is being accurately maintained, the exact number of units sold can easily be determined.

The information should be recorded on a cost projection sheet, illustrated in Figure 23.

The figures listed in the "total sales" column are simply projections of what the sales should be if each unit was indeed sold (as opposed to stolen, not charged for, etc.). For bottled beers (Brands A, B, and C in the example) the projected sales would easily be obtained through multiplying the unit sales price by the number of units sold. Projecting the sales that should be realized from a keg of beer (Brand D in the example) is only slightly more difficult. A half keg of beer contains 15½ gallons, which equals 1,984 ounces. Therefore, if an eight ounce glass is being used the keg would ideally pour 248 glasses. If the sales price per glass were one dollar, a full half keg would

COST PROJECTION SHEET

	UNITS SOLD	SALES PRICE	TOTAL SALES	UNIT COST	TOTAL COST
BOTTLED BEERS:					
Brand A	516	1.00	516.00	.256	132.09
Brand B	309	1.00	309.00	.241	74.47
Brand C	155	1.75	271.25	.366	99.28
KEG BEERS:					
Brand D	2½	248.00	620.00	$26.00	65.00
		TOTALS:	1716.25		370.84

FIGURE 23

theoretically be worth $248.00 in sales.

The figures listed in the "total cost" column are the actual costs incurred, and were obtained by simply multiplying the unit cost by the units sold. The cost of a half keg of Brand D beer is $26.00.

By adding the total sales figures and the total cost figures a total *beer percentage cost* can be determined as follows:

$$\text{P.C.} = \frac{\text{Total Cost}}{\text{Total Sales}} = \frac{370.84}{1,716.25}$$

$$= .2161 \quad \text{or} \quad \underline{21.61\%}$$

This figure is a relatively accurate projection of what the total beer P.C. should have been. The only variable is associated with the projected keg sales. Because of the design of most kegs, they do not yield 100 percent of their contents, and as a result there will be a very small percentage of beer remaining in the keg that cannot be sold. Also, because there are often factors that cause pressure to build in the lines, another small percentage of beer might be lost as foam.

To compensate for the losses incurred through these uncontrollable factors, a manager might allow for a five percent loss when projecting the keg beer sales. In the example, that loss would amount to $31.00 (.05 × 620.00 = 31.00), and as a result the total projected sales would be reduced to $1,685.25 (1,716.25 − 31.00). Based on these sales the adjusted projection of the total beer percentage cost would be 22.00 percent. The actual percentage cost should be very close to this figure.

Wine Cost

Analyzing the wine cost is done in a manner very similar to analyzing beer costs, through projecting a percentage cost based on proportionate sales and comparing it to the actual percentage cost.

The only variable to consider before projecting a wine cost is associated with house wines. The cost per ounce of house wines is easily calculated, but the percentage markup will usually vary considerably based on whether the wine is sold by the glass, half liter, or liter. This is clearly illustrated in the example below.

COST:

House Wines	Gallon Cost	Ounce Cost
Red	$18.50	3.61¢
White	18.00	3.52
Rose	17.85	3.49

SALES PRICE:

Glass (8 oz.)	$1.25
Half Liter (16.9 oz.)	2.25
Liter (33.8 oz.)	4.00

PERCENTAGE COST:

House Wines	Glass	Half Liter	Liter
Red	23.10	27.12	30.50
White	22.53	26.44	29.74
Rose	22.34	26.21	29.49

Notice that the percentage costs vary only slightly between the wines, but radically between the sizes. Therefore, before a realistic projection can be calculated, a determination will have to be made of the ratio of sales between the three sizes of house wine. A very accurate ratio can be determined through either reviewing the distribution of sales on the food servers' checks or by simply having the bartenders keep a log of the various sales for about one week.

Once the ratio has been determined (in this case, 1-6-12), the average percentage cost of each house wine can be calculated as follows:

RED WINE:

Ratio of Sales		Size Percentage Cost		
1 Liter	×	30.50	=	30.50
6 Half Liters	×	27.12	=	162.72
12 Glasses	×	23.10	=	277.20
19				470.42

$$\frac{470.42}{19} = 24.76\%$$

The same count of sales should be used in the calculation of the average percentage cost of each wine, although in this case the size percentage cost will vary.

Because the average percentage cost of the house red wine is 24.76%, and the cost per gallon is $18.50, one gallon of house red wine should yield an average sales of $74.72, as illustrated below.

$$\text{Sales} = \frac{\text{Cost}}{\text{P.C.}} = \frac{18.50}{0.2476} = \$74.72$$

Once a sales projection for each gallon of house wine has been calculated, a total wine percentage cost can be projected in the identical manner that the total beer percentage cost was projected. A simple cost projection sheet is illustrated in Figure 24. A restaurant which stocks a large variety of wines would use an extended projection sheet, but the calculations would remain the same.

$$\text{Percentage Cost} = \frac{1,645.38}{6,106.04} = .2695 \quad \text{or} \quad 26.95\%$$

On the cost projection sheet in Figure 24, the opened gallons of house wines were estimated to the nearest tenth.

The projected total wine percentage cost of 26.95 percent should be very close to the actual percentage cost. The only variable, that of the sales of the various sizes of house wines, should affect the projected cost very little.

COST PROJECTION SHEET

	UNITS SOLD	SALES PRICE	TOTAL SALES	UNIT COST	TOTAL COST
BOTTLED WINES:					
Cabernet Sauvignon	10	10⁰⁰	100⁰⁰	5 75	57 50
Cabernet (Half Bottle)	17	6 50	110 50	3 00	51 50
Pinot Noir	12	8⁰⁰	96 00	4 11	49 32
Gamay Rose	14	7⁰⁰	98⁰⁰	2 95	41 30
Chenin Blanc	12	7 50	90⁰⁰	3 09	37 08
Chenin (Half Bottle)	24	4 75	114 00	1 94	46 56
Pouilly-Fuisse	6	12⁰⁰	84 00	6 18	37 08
Champagne	2	15⁰⁰	30 00	7 28	14 56
Champagne (Half Bottle)	4	8 50	34 00	3.91	15 64
HOUSE WINES:					
Red	15.8	74.75	1181 05	18 50	292 30
White	31.5	74 57	2348 96	18 00	567 00
Rose	24.4	74 59	1820 00	17 85	435 54
			TOTALS: 6106 51		1645 38

FIGURE 24

Liquor Cost

Projecting a realistic liquor cost is very difficult, even with the use of a computerized cash register system. There are simply too many variables involved. Therefore, when analyzing the liquor cost, instead of attempting to determine exactly what the percentage cost should be, it is more realistic for managers to center their attention on broader issues, such as the general distribution of sales and the effects of price variations.

The Distribution of Sales

One effective method of analyzing the distribution of sales involves the study of three general categories of liquor: well liquor, call liquor, and premium call liquor and liqueurs. The cost of cordials (domestic liqueurs) and fortified wines are usually relatively minimal, and need not be considered in this phase of liquor cost analysis.

As a general rule, the average percentage cost of well liquor is very low, that of call liquor slightly higher, and premium call liquor and liqueurs even higher. Exactly how much the percentage cost varies between categories depends upon the price structure and portioning policies of the individual bar. In the example below, each portion equals 1½ ounces and the average portion cost is based on the average cost of 1½ ounces of liquor within each category.

	Sales Price	Average Portion Cost	Average P.C.
Well Liquor	$1.75	22.7¢	12.97%
Call Liquor	2.00	37.7	18.85
Premium Call Liquor and Liqueurs	2.25	57.5	25.64

Because of the differences in the average percentage costs, the sales trends for each category will directly affect the total liquor percentage cost. If, for example, the percentage of well liquor sales increases, the total liquor percentage cost should decrease. On the other hand, if the percentage of premium call liquor and liqueur sales increases, the total liquor percentage cost will also increase.

A simple means of staying aware of changes in the distribution of sales is through counting the number of bottles sold each month and then determining the percentage of bottles sold within each category, as illustrated below.

	Bottles Sold	Percentage
Well Liquor	347	68.44
Call Liquor	129	25.44
Premium Call Liquor and Liqueurs	31	6.11
	507	

$$\text{Well Liquor} = \frac{347}{507} = .6844 \text{ or } 68.44\%$$

$$\text{Call Liquor} = \frac{129}{507} = .2544 \text{ or } 25.44\%$$

$$\text{Premium Call Liquor and Liqueurs} = \frac{31}{507} = .0611 \text{ or } 6.11\%$$

Through calculating these percentages each month, a manager can stay aware of any changes in the distribution of sales and, as a result, be able to determine not only if the total liquor percentage cost will change but, if so, in what direction it will be moving.

Price Variations

Some bars will alter their prices at various intervals throughout the day. For example, the regular prices may be lowered during the cocktail hour to promote business, then raised during the period in which live entertainment is featured to recoup the cost of the entertainment. Because these price variations will dramatically affect the percentage cost of the liquor sales, the sales which occur during these periods should be recorded on a daily basis. Then, at the end of each month the manager should analyze the total sales within each period and determine what effect those sales will have on the liquor cost.

Below is an example of one bar's distribution of sales for one month.

	Sales	Percentage
Cocktail hour sales	3,536.57	12.7
Regular sales	14,313.36	51.4
Entertainment sales	9,997.03	35.9

Because the bar in the example offers lower prices during a cocktail hour, an increase in the percentage of cocktail hour sales will cause an increase in the total liquor percentage cost. Prices during entertainment, being higher than normal, will have just the opposite effect. If the percentage of entertainment sales increases, the total liquor percentage cost would decrease.

Some establishments also apply these price variations to the sales of beer and house wine, but because liquor sales are normally far greater than either beer or house wine sales, the price variations will have the greatest effect on liquor cost.

The Liquor Cost Analysis Sheet

Figure 25 is an example of how a liquor cost analysis sheet should be used. When completed, the sheet should give the manager an excellent perspective of the variables affecting liquor cost. The figures were taken from a bar that

LIQUOR COST ANALYSIS SHEET

Month: JANUARY

Total Sales: 48,728.50

Date	Cocktail Hour	Entertainment
1/1	124.10	—
1/2	132.70	690.15
1/3	165.90	820.10
1/4	185.15	875.85
1/5	328.85	1,931.95
1/6	—	1,520.25
1/7	—	—
1/8	105.00	—
1/9	115.95	608.75
1/10	171.50	715.80
1/11	161.30	765.50
1/12	285.65	1,841.15
1/13	—	1,479.45
1/14	—	—
1/15	147.10	—
1/16	128.35	515.25
1/17	208.90	655.30
1/18	195.55	709.45
1/19	372.85	1,785.20
1/20	—	1,459.90
1/21	—	—
1/22	133.40	—
1/23	152.70	629.80
1/24	175.90	608.40
1/25	225.80	775.55
1/26	341.60	1,695.40
1/27	—	1,328.80
1/28	—	—
1/29	115.70	—
1/30	147.10	545.20
1/31	181.75	808.15

Total 4302.80 22,765.35

Sales Breakdown:

	Sales	Percentage
Cocktail Hour	4,302.80	8.83
Entertainment	22,765.35	46.72
Regular	21,660.35	44.45

Sales Distribution:

	Bottles	Percentage
Well Liquor	637	70.31
Call Liquor	228	25.17
Premium Call and Liqueurs	41	4.52

FIGURE 25

promoted a cocktail hour on Monday through Friday, and live entertainment on Tuesday through Saturday.

If the actual liquor cost should rise, and the liquor cost analysis sheet reflects no reason for the increase, the problem is normally related to poor personnel management.

Food Supply Cost

The non-alcoholic food items used in the bar (mixes and garnishes) are almost exclusively related to liquor sales, and have little to do with either beer or wine sales. Therefore, the actual cost of the food items will usually be equal to an established percentage of liquor sales. That percentage will differ from bar to bar, depending upon the variety of drinks sold, but once a bar's percentage has been calculated it will usually stay relatively consistent each month.

For example, if one month a bar's total liquor sales equaled $20,000 and the cost of food items used equaled $600.00, the cost of the food items used would equal 3.00 percent of the liquor sales. Because this percentage should remain stable, if the next month's liquor sales climbed to $25,000 the manager would be able to realistically project that the cost of the food items will be close to $750.00 (25,000 × .03). Remember, this $25,000 represents only the liquor sales and does not include the sales of either beer or wine.

COST CONTROLS

Cost controls are the final aspect of sales costs we will study. If, once calculated and analyzed, the various sales costs are found to be running too high, the manager will have to either implement new cost control techniques or tighten those controls currently in use.

Actually, cost controls are no more than employee controls. It is the actions of the employees—bartenders, cocktail servers, and food servers—that will determine if the percentage costs are what they should be. Therefore, effective cost controls begin with effective employee training programs, which themselves begin with good hiring policies. The tremendous majority of cost control problems will immediately be eliminated if management consistently looks for the traits of honesty, integrity, and sincere motivation within each new employee.

Detailed training programs will eliminate the majority of the losses that occur through needless mistakes. When new employees are taught a sound working system, they are less often confused and, as a result, the number of careless mistakes will almost disappear.

Before new employees can be trained in cost controls, firm rules pertaining to the areas of portion controls and accounting will have to be established.

Portion Control

Portion control is achieved through first establishing sound measuring procedures and then standardizing recipes.

Generally speaking, there are three ways in which bartenders measure liquor: by free pouring, using a measuring glass, or using an automatic liquor dispenser.

Free Pouring

Most bartenders prefer to measure drinks through free pouring. This is a practice in which no measuring device is used, the bartender simply pours the liquor straight into the glass and estimates the portion based on experience. Many bartenders enjoy doing this because they say it enables them to pour faster and their customers feel they are getting better drinks. As far as portion controls are concerned, these bartenders will explain that because of their experience they're able to pour very accurately simply through "feel" or eyesight.

Unfortunately, this is a common misconception enjoyed mainly by either inexperienced bartenders or otherwise experienced bartenders who are not proficient in using a measuring glass. From a management standpoint, free pouring is the absolute worst method of measuring liquor, especially when the bartender is busy. Even when the bar is slow there is no consistency because no two bartenders free pour identical measurements. During busy periods, a single bartender's pouring will not be consistent with itself, if for no other reason than that the speed of pouring spouts will differ, making consistently accurate free pouring measurements almost impossible.

The argument that customers perfer bartenders to free pour is usually very exaggerated. If the portions are going to be the same, why should the customer care?

Using a Measuring Glass

Measuring liquor with a measuring glass, or jigger, is far superior to simply free pouring. Jiggers are usually either 3/4 ounce or 7/8 ounce in size and are specifically designed to allow the bartender to pour with both speed and accuracy. The bartender fills the jigger and then in one motion pours the contents into the glass while finishing the measurement with a slight free pour (as illustrated in Chapter 5 under "Tools of the Trade"). Even though there is a small degree of free pouring involved, a bartender will be much more consistent in portioning when using a jigger than when simply free pouring.

The most exact method of measuring liquor is through the elimination of all free pouring and the use of a number of lined shot glasses. If, for example, all liquors were to be served in 1¼ ounce portions and all liqueurs exactly one ounce, two shot glasses would be used—one with a 1¼ ounce line, and one with a one ounce line. Smaller portions would be either measured in the smaller shot glass or in a third shot glass with a half ounce line. Under such a program no portion of liquor, liqueur, or fortified wine would be served without first being measured, regardless of how small the quantity.

Unfortunately, such an exacting system greatly inhibits the bartender's efficiency and, as a result, often more is lost in sales through slow service than money saved through added controls.

Possibly the most practical method of portion control involves using the best aspects of each policy. By having the bartender measure all liquor with a jigger, the manager can be assured of both consistent portioning and adequate speed. By insisting that all liqueurs be measured with a lined shot glass, the manager can be assured that the most expensive items are being measured with the greatest possible accuracy. Finally, by allowing the bartender to free pour vermouths and mixes the manager can increase the bartender's speed at very little expense.

Automatic Liquor Dispensers

Portioning well liquor through an automatic liquor dispensing system is not the complete answer to portion control, but it does have its advantages. When a quality dispensing system is properly adjusted, the bartender will be able to pour with a great deal of speed and accuracy. Also, because it will usually be possible to purchase the liquor dispensed through the system in either gallon or half gallon sizes, as opposed to quarts, the manager will normally be able to enjoy a lower cost per ounce.

Unfortunately, there are also disadvantages in the use of such a system, the largest of which are poor customer acceptance and high installation cost. As a rule, customers seem to prefer seeing both the bottle from which the liquor is being poured and the portion being measured by the bartender.

Because most automatic dispensing systems dispense only well liquors, the bartender will still be responsible for measuring the more expensive items—call liquors and liqueurs. Therefore, it is best for management to think of such systems primarily as a means of increasing their bartenders' speed without sacrificing accuracy in portioning, but not as the answer to all portion control problems.

Pouring Spouts and Glassware

There are a few secondary factors pertaining to portion controls that a manager should also consider. Pouring spouts, for example, can be purchased on the basis of their speed. Bartenders normally prefer steel pouring spouts with wide mouths because they dispense liquor very rapidly, but from a management standpoint it is a better policy to use slower pouring spouts. Even though such pouring spouts might slightly inhibit the efficiency of the bartender, they will provide the bartender with a great deal more control over the flow of liquor and will result in a considerable saving of expense.

The size of glassware is also important and should depend upon a bar's specific portioning policies. If, for example, management prefers relatively light portioning, a large rock glass will defeat their policies by encouraging bartenders to overpour, since bartenders naturally like to please their customers by serving drinks that appear to be full. Large ice cubes have the same effect—because of their bulk, only a limited number will fit into a rock glass and will therefore displace only a limited amount of space. As a result, a large amount of liquor will be needed to fill the glass. On the other hand, the same glass completely filled with smaller ice cubes can appear to be full when far less liquor has been added. The larger number of smaller ice cubes will simply displace more space within the glass.

Standardized Recipes

The second phase of portion controls involves standardizing recipes. Obviously, it will be impossible to control portions if each bartender uses a different recipe to prepare the same cocktail. Therefore, it is very important for management to make it mandatory that all drinks be prepared in an identical manner. The only way to guarantee this is through creating a list of recipes, issuing a copy of the list to each bartender, and establishing a firm rule that only those recipes be used.

Accounting

After establishing rules pertaining to portion controls, the manager should next establish a detailed record-keeping system to guarantee that all sales, checks, and cash will be accounted for on a daily basis. Such a system should be based on the following three general policies:

1) No item (straight liquor, mixed drink, beer or wine) should either be served by the bartender or issued to a food or cocktail server without being accounted for.

2) All cash register transactions should be recorded on checks.

3) All checks (bartenders', food servers', and cocktail servers') should be counted and audited daily.

Items served from the bar can be accounted for through the use of the Bar service/Service paid system described in Chapter Five or one similar to it while the system used for check and cash controls should be similar to the system outlined in Chapter Nine under "Cocktail Servers."

For such a system to succeed, the rules will have to be very detailed and all employees will have to be well trained and completely aware of their responsibilities. It is also best to have the check counting and auditing responsibilities assigned to either a specific assistant manager or a single, very trustworthy, employee. To assure proper controls, a minimum of two hours each day should be allocated for the sole purpose of auditing the previous day's checks. Even though this time might initially appear to the manager to be costly, the returns attributed to such controls will be substantial.

The bookkeeper should maintain at least two logs, one of used checks and one of employee mistakes.

WEEKLY CHECK LOG

Bartenders:

Date:	M 7/2	T 7/3	W 7/4	Th 7/5	F 7/6	S 7/7	Su 7/8
SUE ADAMS	411512 / 411520	411531 / 411544	411550 / 411569	411570 / 411584	411585 / 411599	OFF	OFF
MIKE BROWN	387904 / 387914	OFF	OFF	387915 / 387931	387931 / 387957	387972 / 387981	387982 / 387992
JOHN FARMER	OFF	OFF	OFF	OFF	430015 / 430028	430029 / 430051	OFF
JUDY JONES	475102 / 475112	475113 / 475120	475121 / 475133	475134 / 475148	475149 / 475163	OFF	OFF
PETE NORTH	OFF	463334 / 463341	463342 / 463361	463362 / 463371	463371 / 463391	463391 / 463394	OFF
DEBBIE PALMER	476002 / 476008	476009 / 476014	476015 / 476028	OFF	OFF	476039 / 476041	476042 / 476061
DAN WILLIAMS	OFF	OFF	OFF	OFF	OFF	495050 / 495070	495071 / 495084

Cocktail Servers:

	M 7/2	T 7/3	W 7/4	Th 7/5	F 7/6	S 7/7	Su 7/8
MARY EDWARDS	2851 / 2864	2865 / 2881	2882 / 2908	2909 / 2935	2936 / 2959	OFF	OFF
JEAN FRANKLIN	OFF	4712 / 4729	4730 / 4756	4757 / 4789	4790 / 4823	4824 / 4853	OFF
CHRIS MONROE	7820 / 7834	OFF	OFF	7835 / 7852	7853 / 7871	7871 / 7902	7903 / 7918
TERRY O'DELL	OFF	OFF	OFF	OFF	OFF	6241 / 6258	6259 / 6274
KIM MILLER	8147 / 8150	8151 / 8163	8164 / 8179	8180 / 8194	8195 / 8219	OFF	OFF

FIGURE 26

EMPLOYEE RECORD BOOK

JOHN JOHNSON

DATE

2 / 13	CHECK #091534 MISSING	
3 / 22	CASH SHORT $12.50	
5 / 17	CHECK #091953 $10.00 ERROR IN ADDITION	
8 / 9	CASH SHORT $16.00	
8 / 15	CHECK #092392 MISSING	

FIGURE 27

The *weekly check log* sheet (shown in Figure 26) keeps a daily record of all of the checks used by each employee. After verifying that no checks are missing, the bookkeeper should record the beginning and ending numbers of the used checks in the weekly check log. Through such records, the bookkeeper can verify that the starting number of each day's checks is in numerical sequence with the previous day's ending number. This procedure prevents the disappearance of an employee's first or last check going unnoticed.

After each employee's checks have been audited, any major mistakes should be logged in an *employee record book* (Figure 27). Each employee should be assigned a page within the record book and each day's major mistakes should be recorded under the responsible employee's name. Items such as missing checks and cash register errors exceeding $5.00 should be considered major mistakes.

After management of employees has been tightened by establishing firm portion control rules and a detailed accounting system, the following managerial procedures should be implemented to complete a sound cost control program.

Scheduled Physical Inventories

A complete physical inventory should be taken at least once each month—preferably twice each month. If the bar and storeroom are properly organized, a complete physical inventory of all liquor, beer, wine, and food items should take less than one hour and, if the itemized sales and purchasing records have been accurately maintained, it should be possible to extend the inventory and calculate itemized sales costs within an hour and a half. This way, by expending no more than five hours each month, a manager can be aware of the actual itemized sales costs each fifteen days. Under such a system the costs can never get too far out of line without the manager realizing it almost immediately.

Calculating Daily Pouring Costs

Pouring cost can be determined relatively accurately on a daily basis by keeping a daily log of the total value of all of the used inventory listed on the daily requisition sheet. An estimated pouring cost can be calculated through dividing the total cost of the requisitioned inventory by the day's sales.

The variable in this system is the opened or "working" inventory, located in the display cases and well areas. The actual value of this inventory will vary each day. Each time an ounce of liquor is poured, the value of the working inventory will drop, though when a bottle is emptied it will be replaced with a full bottle and the value of the working inventory will rise. The question becomes how much the value of the working inventory will vary from day to day, on the average? A realistic answer can be determined by following these three steps:

1) Determine the cost of the entire working inventory, as if each bottle were

full. This includes every bottle that will be stored open in each display case and well area in the bar.

2) Divide that figure by two. The result will be equal to the average value of the working inventory.

3) Multiply the remaining figure by 0.10. It would be unrealistic to expect the value of the working inventory to vary more than 10% from its average level. Therefore, by multiplying the value of the average working inventory by 0.10, the manager can derive a figure equaling the maximum amount by which the working inventory might vary.

The best way to clarify these points is through an example. Figure 28 shows a record of a bar's daily sales and the daily value of the inventory listed on the daily requisition sheet. The percentage cost in the right hand column is taken from the accumulated totals, and was derived by dividing the total cost to date by the total sales to date.

Based on the value of the used inventory for the week, the pouring cost was determined to be 19.09 percent. The question the bar manager should ask is, how accurate is the cost figure? Because the only variable is related to the working inventory, the answer to that question can be determined through following the three steps listed above. Using the same bar as in Figure 28 as an example, it would be done this way:

1) The bar in the example has two identically stocked display cases, each with a full bottle inventory equaling $423.71, and two well areas, each

DAILY REQUISITION SHEET
LISTING SALES AND INVENTORY

| DATE | SALES | | COST | | |
	DAILY	TOTAL	DAILY	TOTAL	PERCENTAGE
8 2	628 30	628 30	126 10	126 10	24.82
8 3	754 15	1382 45	100 83	226 93	16.41
8 4	897 45	2279 90	192 81	419 73	18.41
8 5	871 90	3151 80	140 24	559 97	17.76
8 6	1584 85	4736 65	325 51	885 48	18.69
8 7	1273 95	6010 60	257 70	1143 18	19.02
8 8	709 05	6719 65	139 71	1282 89	19.09
		6719 65		1282 89	19.09

FIGURE 28

stocked with a full bottle inventory equaling $32.76. Therefore, if each bottle in the bar's entire working inventory were full, the cost would equal $912.94.

2) The average value of the working inventory would be $456.47 (912.94 ÷ 2).

3) Because the value of the actual working inventory should not vary by more than 10 percent of the value of the average working inventory, the total cost figure should not be off by more than $45.65 ($456.47 × .10).

With these figures, the manager can conclude that the total cost figure should be no higher than $1,328.57 (1,282.89 + 45.65) and no lower than $1,237.21 (1,282.89 − 45.65). Through calculating the percentage cost using each of these figures, a range can be established within which the actual pouring cost should fall.

Highest possible percentage cost:

$$\frac{1,328.57}{6,719.65} = \underline{19.77\%}$$

Lowest possible percentage cost:

$$\frac{1,237.21}{6,719.65} = \underline{18.41\%}$$

The benefit of using this system is that the manager will be able to make a very realistic determination of the pouring cost without taking a physical inventory. Even though in the example the manager's estimate was only within a range of 1.36 percent (19.77 − 18.41), these figures were derived from only one week's sales. As the sales increase, the margin of error will continually decrease and, as a result, the manager's estimates will become more exact.

It must be remembered that the pouring cost does not include the cost of the non-alcoholic food items used. That cost will have to be estimated, based on past records, and added to these figures to estimate the total sales cost figure. If the cost of food items had been running at 1.8 percent of total sales, the manager could estimate the total sales percentage cost in the example week as falling between 20.21% (18.41 + 1.8) and 21.57% (19.77 + 1.8).

Utilizing Spotters

The final, and by far the most effective means of detecting either employee mistakes or theft, is through the utilization of trained spotters, persons who sit at the bar posing as customers while actually observing the actions of all employees. Trained, competent spotters can be a tremendous aid to management, but untrained spotters have the habit of creating more problems than they observe.

It is best to hire only spotters who are themselves capable bartenders, and to use them only after they've thoroughly memorized the following:

1) Sales prices of all alcoholic beverages
2) Rules pertaining to portion controls
3) Rules pertaining to the accounting system
4) General house policies

Chapter 4

MERCHANDISING

Today the field of merchandising is becoming an increasingly large part of bar management. Regardless of how well costs are controlled, a bar will never realize its profit potential through controls alone. Increased competition and continually increasing costs mean that a bar must continually utilize profitable merchandising techniques to obtain optimum sales.

Besides being aware of successful merchandising techniques, a bar manager must also know how to analyze those techniques in terms of cost, potential sales, and potential profit. Only with this knowledge, coupled with sound employee management, can a successful merchandising campaign be sustained.

THE FOUNDATION OF SUCCESSFUL MERCHANDISING

Merchandising, like most aspects of bar management, begins with employee training. All employees must realize that they are expected to be more than order takers and servants; they are expected to be professional salespersons, who are trained by management and earn commissions in the form of added tips. This is a concept that management must continually stress, because most new employees will have never before been required to do much more than the simple manual labor associated with customer service. All employees must realize that their level of performance will have to improve, to meet rising costs and tougher competition. They will now have to become professionals, especially within the area of selling skills.

It must be emphasized that merchandising techniques such as table tents, wine lists, cocktail hours, and hors d'oeuvres will increase sales on their own, but to achieve the full potential sales increase, these techniques must be promoted by the employees. Bartenders must point out the quality of the hors d'oeuvres, food servers must call customers' attention to the table tents, cocktail servers must inform their customers of the lower prices being offered during the cocktail hour, and the hosts or hostesses must, after seating customers, properly present the wine list.

If all employees realize and accept their sales responsibilities, management will find that virtually any merchandising technique will succeed. For this reason, successful merchandising always begins with employee training.

THE MATHEMATICS OF MERCHANDISING

Before implementing any merchandising techniques an astute manager will first thoroughly analyze the costs involved, specifically the break-even point (how much the sales will have to increase to simply pay for the costs of the techniques). The answer to that question can be determined by using the following formula:

$$\text{Needed Sales Increase} = \frac{\text{Total Cost}}{\text{Gross Percentage Markup}}$$

The *total cost* figure should represent all of the costs incurred in the actual creation and usage of the merchandising technique. The *gross percentage markup* is derived by simply subtracting the sales percentage cost of the item(s) being merchandised from 100 percent. For example, if a bottle of wine is being promoted that has a percentage cost of 30 per cent, the percentage markup will be 70 percent.

If, for example, a manager was considering printing table flyers to promote the sale of a special house drink, the only costs involved would be related to art work, the actual printing cost, and possibly the cost of plastic stands into which the flyers would be inserted. The total cost might be as follows:

$$
\begin{aligned}
\$ \ 25.00 &\ — \ \text{Art Work} \\
40.50 &\ — \ \text{Printing} \\
\underline{45.24} &\ — \ \text{Plastic Stands} \\
\text{Total Cost} = \$110.74 &
\end{aligned}
$$

If the percentage cost of the house drink was 22.68 percent, the gross percentage markup would be 77.32 percent. Using this figure and the total cost figure, the manager could calculate that an increase in sales of $143.22 would be needed simply to pay for the initial costs:

$$\text{Needed Sales Increase} = \frac{110.74}{.7732} = \$143.22$$

This figure represents the needed *increase* in sales, the sales over and above what normally would have incurred without the use of the flyers.

Next, the manager should make an estimate of how much the sales will increase and how much profit can realistically be expected. This figure can be calculated using the following formula:

Gross Profit = (Sales Increase − Total Cost) × Gross Percentage Markup

If the manager in the example planned on using the table flyers for six weeks, and estimated that the flyers would increase sales at the rate of $100.00 each week, the gross profit that would be realized after the six week period would be calculated as follows:

$$\text{Gross Profit} = (\$600.00 - \$110.74) \times .7732$$
$$= \$489.26 \times .7732 = \underline{\$378.30}$$

Before making these calculations, the total cost figure should be thoroughly analyzed, because there are often a number of secondary costs that can easily be overlooked. For example, if a manager were considering boosting sales on the usually quiet Monday nights by featuring live entertainment, there would be more costs involved than simply the employment of the entertainers. To insure that the added customers are well served, management may need to add a second bartender, one or two more cocktail servers, and possibly a door person. There will also be secondary costs related to the added wear on carpets and furnishings, advertising, and general maintenance. On a daily basis many of these costs may seem trivial, but they do exist and eventually they will have to be paid for. A manager should analyze merchandising techniques from strictly a business standpoint and therefore consider every cost that will or even might occur.

MERCHANDISING TECHNIQUES

An almost unlimited number of techniques can be used to increase bar sales. Some of the most successful will be discussed in the following pages. Regardless of the actual number of techniques employed, their success will depend upon the imagination and creativity of the manager. Through simply advertising a seasonal drink on a table tent, the sales of that drink will increase, but, as the old saying goes, "No one likes to be sold, but everyone likes to buy." This is especially true when the item for sale has unusual or unique qualities. If the manager, using a little creativity, printed on the table tent the interesting history behind the drink, the sales might double instead of only slightly increasing—at no extra cost!

The merchandising techniques presented on the following pages should be analyzed with an open mind. Most of these techniques have been used for a number of years, but with the addition of a little imagination, they can continue to be used with great success.

The remainder of the chapter is divided into two categories of merchandising: wine merchandising and liquor merchandising.

Wine Merchandising
Selecting and Pricing Wines

The establishment's policies and practices in selecting and pricing wines will have major importance when it comes to merchandising the wine. Many details of wine selection have already been discussed in Chapter One, under "Wine Purchasing." In tying in wine purchasing with merchandising, the key points to remember are:

Always select wines with regard to the desires of the specific clientele of the establishment. The wine list should feature wines customers are familiar with, will enjoy, and can afford.

Medium price and less expensive restaurants will find that the actual number of wines stocked is not nearly as important as some wine salespeople might imply. In most instances, a manager will find that stocking an extensive variety is an expensive and seldom profitable means of increasing wine sales. What often happens in such situations is that the least popular wines sit in wine racks for months and sometimes years. Stocking a huge variety of wines should be thought of as no more than a merchandising technique, a means of possibly increasing wine sales. Unfortunately, only a small percentage of restaurants, usually the most expensive, have found this technique to be successful.

A small, imaginative selection of wines is always more profitable than a large, poor selection of wines.

Management should always keep an open ear to customer requests, and at least once a year rewrite the wine list. The least popular selections and those that are out of stock should be deleted, while currently popular selections should be added.

Even when offering only a small selection of wines, management can still offer customers a changing roster of alternatives through featuring a "Wine of the Month" or a small "Reserve Selection" of wines which can be presented upon request.

Wines are often grossly overpriced, and today's customers both realize it and resent it. It is curious that some restaurants insist on insulting their customers instead of pleasing them by allowing them to enjoy a reasonably priced bottle of wine with their meal. Management will find that selling a great deal of wine with only a 40 percent markup will prove to be far more profitable than selling very little wine with a 70 percent markup. Not only will the restaurant make more money through the added wine sales, but more importantly, customers will better enjoy their visits and return more often.

Bottled wine prices should not be established solely through the use of a standard markup policy, such as double wholesale. Each wine should be judged on its own and priced in a manner that will assure a steady rate of sales. Wines that don't sell are usually either overpriced or not well known. Regardless of the reason, such wines represent tied up capital.

Customer satisfaction should always be the primary consideration in the selection and pricing of wine. Wine popularity is continually growing in the United States and restaurants can take best advantage of the situation through offering their customers an enjoyable, reasonably priced selection. Extensive selections of high priced wines have the tendency to intimidate and aggravate more customers than they please.

Designing a Wine List

From a merchandising standpoint, the actual design and arrangement of the wine list is very important. A properly designed wine list will significantly add to the sales of bottled wines, especially to customers inexperienced in wine buying. When making a decision on design, the following aspects of the list should be considered.

The Cover

As a general rule, the more attractively covered the wine list is, the better. The customer should feel that the selection of wine is an important part of the meal, and an attractive wine list will support that feeling. Inexpensive, lightweight wine lists have the psychological effect of downplaying the importance of wine. Such lists give the customer the impression that selecting the wine is no more than an afterthought and relatively unimportant.

Though the cover should be attractive, it does not have to be similar to the heavy leather bindings found in many of the more expensive restaurants. Management can, and should, use a little creativity in this area. One restaurant reported increased wine sales after creating wine list covers from beautiful laminated photographs of bottled wines and grapes. The photographs were so well done that customers found themselves almost forced to pick up the wine lists for a closer look.

Listing the Wines

The variety, producer, vintage, shipper, size, and cost of each bottle of wine should be listed on the wine list. Some restaurants will drop the vintage, and others will even neglect to list the producer. They do this to avoid the cost involved in reprinting wine lists. By simply listing the size and type of wine a number of substitutions can be made. Inexperienced wine drinkers might find this policy acceptable, but experienced wine drinkers will find it intolerable. Some will simply refuse to order wine rather than go through the aggravation of asking the food server a number of questions.

It is a far better policy to have the wine list reprinted each year. Not only can the wine list be brought up to date to reflect current prices, but the slowest moving wines can be replaced with more popular selections. Customers will enjoy a fresh selection, and the added sales will easily pay for the printing costs.

Another good policy is to list wines by numbers, which are sometimes referred to as bin numbers. This policy will allow inexperienced wine drinkers to order wine by the number and thereby avoid the embarrassment of having to pronounce an unfamiliar name.

Descriptions

Each selection of wine should be followed by a detailed, yet clearly understandable description. Experienced wine drinkers will enjoy the detail, while inexperienced wine drinkers will enjoy the clarity. After describing the wine itself, brief reference might be given on the type of food for which the wine is best suited.

Inexperienced wine drinkers should find the descriptions an aid in making their selection. A brief discription such as, "A fruity wine with distinctive flavor" leaves quite a bit to the imagination, and would definitely not add to the sales of that wine.

Special Selections

One means of extending the wine list is by noting on the list that the restaurant also offers a small stock of "Reserve Selections," which will be identified upon request. These wines should be of especially fine quality and should be stocked to offer something for the more selective wine drinker.

Whenever the manager has the opportunity to purchase a particularly fine wine at an unusually good price, the purchase should be made and the wine added to the inventory of "Reserve Selections." These selections should consist of no more than two to four wines. There need only be a limited inventory on them.

Presenting the Wine List

The way in which a wine list is presented to the customer will have a significant effect on wine sales. In fact, to inexperienced wine drinkers, the presentation of the wine list itself can be more persuasive than the actual list of wines.

The absolute worst method of presenting a wine list is to do so only upon customer request. It is only slightly better to use the wine list as a centerpiece for each table or to list the selection of bottled wines on the menu.

The wine list must be "presented" in a manner at least as formal as that used to present the menus. The most common practice is to have the wine list presented by the host or hostess to the host of the party, immediately after the presentation of the menus. In doing so, the restaurant host or hostess should always bring the wine list to the customer's attention by saying something similar to, "If you care for wine with your meal, here is a list of our selections." From a merchandising standpoint this announcement is very important because it has the effect of making the customer at least consider purchasing a bottle of wine.

Some restaurants have enjoyed added success as a result of making the presentation later, after the customers have had an opportunity to read the menu. In this case, the wine list, instead of being presented by the host or hostess, is presented by the food server, who will usually be more persuasive. After introducing themselves, the food servers first take cocktail orders and then, before leaving the table, present the wine list by laying it close to the host and announcing, "If you would enjoy a bottle of wine this evening, here is a list of our selections." Some restaurant managers prefer that their food servers go one step further by first opening and then handing the opened wine list to the host.

As in all merchandising techniques, imagination is the key. A few very creative restaurants boast of great success through actually doing away with wine lists altogether. Instead of presenting lists, they present the bottles themselves, with each bottle of wine displayed on a beautifully decorated cart, which is rolled to the table.

The presentation of the wine list can be a highly effective merchandising tool. When done properly, a restaurant can realize a tremendous increase in wine sales without any added costs. All that is needed is properly trained employees.

Featuring a Wine of the Month

An excellent means of merchandising wines is by offering customers an unusually good price for a selected "wine of the month," which may or may not be on the wine list. By featuring wines not on the list, management can offer not only an excellent value but added variety as well.

This policy needn't be costly, if the wine selected is one currently being offered by the distributor at a post off discount rate. The savings in purchasing cost can then be passed on to the customer in the form of a lowered sales price. Another profitable idea is to feature one of the slower moving wines on the wine list as the wine of the month. Even though the sales price might have to be significantly reduced, a profit will still be realized and, equally important, a good amount of tied up capital will be released. A secondary benefit of featuring a wine on the wine list is that it will give customers an opportunity to taste the wine, in the hope of boosting sales at a later date.

The wine of the month can easily be advertised on table tents or by attaching an insert to the wine list. Some restaurants have had great success by actually using the wine of the month as a centerpiece for each table. Food servers can then introduce the wine by simply pointing out the bottle. If the customer does not care to order the wine the bottle is then removed.

Selling Bottled Wines by the Glass

As a result of the tremendous increase in wine popularity in the United States, a growing number of restaurants, especially those having only beer and wine licenses, are offering customers the opportunity to purchase quality bottled wines by the glass. Even though the price of a glass of such wines is considerably higher than the average glass price of house wine, an increasing number of customers are finding the superior quality to be worth the added expense.

The key to success in this merchandising technique is in not eliminating the lower priced house wine, but rather adding the more expensive wines, giving the customer an opportunity to make a choice. For example, a restaurant might offer three red wines which may be purchased by the glass; a jug wine at a price of $1.25, and two bottled wines at prices of $1.75 and $2.50. Therefore, when a customer requests a glass of red wine, the food server would have to inquire as to what variety of red wine is desired and inform the customer of the various selections and prices. Employee training will play a critical role in the success of this program. The food servers will have to memorize both the selections and prices of red, white, and rose bottled wines which can be served by the glass.

Bottled House Wines

House wines are generally served by the liter or half liter, but sales can sometimes be increased by improving the quality of the house wine and serving it in bottles and half bottles. Customers will almost always prefer to drink wine from a freshly opened corked bottle rather than from a carafe as long as the price is not prohibitive. In the sale of house wines price is critically important, so a manager who considers switching from gallons to fifths and tenths must avoid too large a price jump.

The goal in implementing such a program should be added profits though increased sales, not an increased profit per sale. For example, if the house wine is currently selling for $4.00 per liter and the cost is $1.35, the gross profit would be $2.65 and the percentage cost would be 33.75 percent (1.35/4.00). If the manager was considering switching to a better quality bottled wine at the cost of $2.35 per fifth, the sales price should be not much higher than $5.00 (2.35 + 2.65). Even though the percentage cost will be higher (2.35/5.00 = 47.00%), the actual gross profit will be the same ($2.65), which would be both fair to the customer and profitable for the manager, who should realize an increase in house wine sales. The key to success is in not attempting to stretch the price too much, as that would result in stiff customer resistance.

An important factor to consider before entering into such a program is the cost of a glass of wine. Glasses will have to be poured from opened bottles at the bar, at a significantly increased cost over jug wine prices. The cost can be passed on to the customer but, again, the manager will have to use caution.

Some restaurants have used this merchandising technique with tremendous success, but for many others, it has failed. What a manager must remember is that even though customers may prefer bottled wines over jug wines, they may be willing to pay only a slightly higher price. Actually, the quality of the restaurant will have a lot to do with the success of this program. Normally medium to higher priced restaurants do much better, while the less expensive establishments are usually better off staying with jug wines.

Wine Displays

Some restaurants have increased their wine sales through doing no more than building wine displays at the entrance and at various locations throughout the dining room. The managers say the displays, which often feature a variety of polished wine bottles, wine racks, sections of wine barrels, glassware, grapes, and draped velvet, enhance the customers' appetite for wine.

Liquor Merchandising

There are two areas of liquor merchandising: dining room sales, the sale of liquor to those who are eating in the restaurant; and bar sales, the sale of liquor to those who are drinking either at the bar or in the cocktail lounge. The manager will have to think of both areas separately and will need to implement different sales techniques to promote sales in each category.

Dining Room Sales

Recipes

The first way to increase liquor sales is through improving the quality of the drinks. Those customers in the dining room are at the restaurant primarily because of the food; as a result, the cost of drinks is not their primary concern. The quality of the drinks will impress these customers far more than a lower price.

Therefore, the manager should continually strive to not only increase the quality of the recipes and mixes, but the garnishes as well. To some customers, appearance means as much as taste; therefore, management should insist that all cocktails are garnished properly and only fresh garnishes are used.

Glassware

Well prepared, lavishly garnished cocktails can still appear relatively ordinary when served in plain glassware. Stocking unique or unusually attractive glassware will result in an increase in cocktail sales and should be considered a merchandising technique.

As with all merchandising techniques, the manager should first determine whether the added cost will guarantee enough added sales to make it profitable. The final decision will be greatly dependent upon the individual bar, but in the majority of instances increasing the quality of glassware will prove profitable.

The Menu

Using a specific section of the food menu to merchandise either liquor or wine is a good merchandising technique, because there is no cost involved. From an aesthetic standpoint, it is best to design the section as tastefully as possible and to promote only one or two ideas.

For example, under the heading of desserts, after all of the desserts have been listed, the following might be added:

—FROM THE LOUNGE—
Cafe Baron

For those of you who would enjoy something different, may we proudly suggest our own house coffee. It's our own secret recipe consisting of a delicious blend of exotic liqueurs and fresh hot coffee, topped with whipped cream!

Under the entrees, the following thought might be included:

A great meal is one which is perfectly complemented with wine. May we suggest you complement your meal with a selection from our famous wine list.

Some restaurants have realized increased wine sales through listing below each entree the wine which would best complement that meal. This technique has worked, but some customers consider it too aggressive an approach, while others are actually offended by advice on which wine to select with their meal.

Table Tents

One of the most common means of promoting liquor sales is through the use of table tents. One large chain of restaurants has had tremendous success in using a wide variety of beautifully colored flyers inserted into attractive plastic stands and set on each table. Unfortunately, multicolored table tents can be extremely expensive to print, and therefore smaller establishments will have to be satisfied with either printing in one color or using only those tents issued by liquor distributors.

The table tents liquor distributors issue are sometimes very attractive, and using them will always prove successful because there is no cost involved. The disadvantage is that they are often used by a number of restaurants and people are used to seeing them. As a result, it will often prove to be more profitable for a restaurant to print its own unique table tents, as they will usually create more interest.

Even though, for economy purposes, it may be best to print in only one color, the loss of color can be compensated for by having the printing done on attractively colored stock and through the use of some attractive, inexpensive, artwork. Examples of flyers that have been proven successful are illustrated in Figures 29-32.

Cocktail List

An interesting companion to the wine list is a cocktail list, which gives customers the opportunity to choose between a wide range of exciting cocktails they might otherwise not have considered.

The idea behind such a list should be to offer something for everyone and every season. To ensure continued success, the cocktail list, like the wine list, should be updated and reprinted each year, with the less popular drinks removed and the drinks currently most popular added.

To add to the success of cocktail lists, food servers should be trained to properly use them. For example, if customers feel they might enjoy cocktails, but are undecided on what to order, the food server might suggest, "Why don't you glance through our cocktail guide and I'll return in one moment." The same response should be used for customers who are considering after-dinner drinks. For the customer who asks if there are any house specialties, the food server should be prepared to highly recommend the two or three most popular requests and finish by saying, "We also have a number of other specialty cocktails listed on our cocktail list."

With regard to presentation, the cocktail list might simply be left standing next to the centerpiece of each table, while the wine list should be more formally presented by either the host, hostess, or food server.

An example of a successful cocktail list is illustrated in Figure 33.

Bar Sales
Featuring a Cocktail Hour

Cocktail hours, sometimes referred to as "happy hours," are periods in which drinks, usually only well drinks, are either sold at a reduced price or

FIGURE 29: Seasonal Table Tents—Summer. This summer flyer promotes not only the classic Mai Tai and the increasingly popular Pina Colada, but a house specialty as well. On a hot summer day how many people could resist enjoying "the excitment of the islands" with a cold and refreshing tropical treat!

Winter Cheer!

GET INTO THE SPIRIT OF THE SEASON
WITH A SPECIAL WINTER TREAT FROM THE LOUNGE

Tom & Jerry
*A Classic Hot Winter Cocktail
Guaranteed to Bring the Spirit Out!*

Hot Buttered Rum
*Always a Favorite, Especially
on Cold Days!*

Brandy Eggnog
(Hot or Cold)
*Hot or Over the Rocks, a Great
Seasonal Treat!*

Hot Brick Toddy
*Cinnamon, Butter, a Pinch of Sugar,
Whiskey and Steaming Hot Water!*

FIGURE 30: Seasonal Table Tents—Winter. Promoting hot winter drinks can be very profitable, but it is an area that many bars neglect. The hot drinks promoted on the "Winter Cheer!" flyer are all easy to prepare and have traditionally proved to be good sellers.

This flyer was very successful, maybe because almost everyone wants to "get into the spirit of the season."

CAPPUCCINO!

The Legendary Cappuccino combines the distinctive flavors of fresh coffee, rich chocolate and a mild mixture of liqueurs.

Although delicious anytime, Cappuccino has always been regarded as an excellent finishing touch to a fine meal.

We've found this famous drink to taste even better when topped with whipped cream and a sprinkle of chocolate curls!

FIGURE 31: Classic Drinks. The "Cappucino!" flyer is an excellent example of how a mildly popular drink can be made very popular with a little imagination and a well-written table tent. The simple idea of adding a "sprinkle of chocolate curls" resulted in a dramatic increase in sales.

BE ADVENTUROUS

Treat Yourself to Something a little Different Today, Like...

BANANA AMARETTO

We Know You'll find this Unique Blend of Amaretto and Fresh Banana to be Quite an Exciting new Taste Treat!

MELON MARGARITA

There's Nothing more Refreshing than an Ice Cold Margarita, Except when you add the Taste of Honey Dew Melon! An Exceptionally Refreshing Drink.

ROOT BEER FLOAT

If You don't really care for the Taste of Liquor, but always Enjoyed the Flavor of a Good Old Fashioned Root Beer Float, THIS IS YOUR DRINK! It's Made with Cola, a Mild Mixture of Liquers and a Dash of Cream and it's Served in a Frosted Mug Topped with Whipped Cream and a Cherry!

FIGURE 32: Unusual Drinks. Unusual drinks are normally good sellers, especially for those who don't care for the harsh taste of straight liquor. Such flyers are also a good means of advertising the versatility and creativity of the bar.

Sunny's
Guide to the Spirits

We at Sunny's have always felt we could greatly enhance the dining experience of many of our customers if we could complement their meal with an unusually fine tasting cocktail. Because of this we've taken great measures to find and use only what we consider to be the finest recipes, mixes and garnishes in preparing each drink.

Also, because we've found that many of our customers enjoyed the excitement of trying different, exotic or unusual tasting cocktails, we've discovered and created a wide variety of deliciously different drinks.

All in all, we've taken great pleasure in trying to reinstill the excitement, color and mystique of the spirits back into our liquor program.

A few of our more popular requests are listed on the following pages, but if you're in the mood for something different, ask your waitress for a list of our Seasonal Specialties!

FIGURE 33

From the Caribbean and South Pacific

For those of you who enjoy the refreshing taste derived from a special mixture of exotic fruits, juices and imported rums, we offer the following delightfully flavored Tropical Cocktails

Island Breeze *It's Sunny's own delicious blend of Tropical Fruits, Juices and Rums. A great favorite among our customers.*

Tahitian Sunset *An exciting combination of Pineapple, Banana, Rum and Grenadine.*

Polynesian Cooler *An exceptionally cool and refreshing cocktail, highlighted with just a hint of mint.*

Mai Tai *"Mai Tai Roa Ae" in Tahitian means "Out of this World. . .the Best." All Mai Tai lovers should try our special recipe for this old favorite.*

Pina Colada *Exotic mixture of Coconut, Pineapple and Rum. For an interesting variation, ask for it with strawberries!*

Treasure Island Special *Enjoy the excitement of the Islands with this delightfully flavored cocktail. It's made with its own special assortment of imported Rums, exotic Liqueurs and Fruit Juices.*

FIGURE 33 (Cont.)

Enjoy

Something Different

Here is quite a selection of unusual treats that we've found to be very popular among our customers.

Melon Margarita *You'll find that a cold Margarita can taste even more refreshing when you add the light and cool taste of Honeydew Melon.*

Banana Amaretto *A unique blend of fresh Banana, Amaretto and a dash of cream. Deliciously different!*

Rootbeer Float *This interesting mixture of liqueurs actually has the flavor of an old fashion Rootbeer float. We even serve it in a frosted mug and top it with whipped cream and a cherry!*

Apricot Sour *A tasty treat for Apricot lovers. A favorite with ladies.*

Bananalua *Our own mixture of Kahlua, Vanilla ice cream, fresh Banana and a mild mixture of liqueurs.*

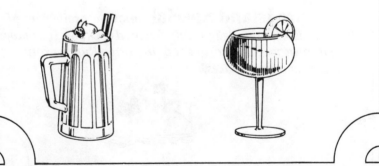

FIGURE 33 (Cont.)

Hot Cheer!

Excellent when it's cold or after any meal.

Sunny's Cafe *Hot black coffee and our own special mixture of liqueurs. Delicious anytime!*

Irish Coffee *A classic mixture of coffee, a pinch of brown sugar and a fine Irish Whiskey.*

Cappuccino *This famous coffee drink is particularly delicious after a fine meal.*

Hot Buttered Rum *Always a favorite on cold days!*

Mexican Coffee *The increasingly popular combination of Tequila, Kahlua and coffee.*

Dutch Coffee *This old favorite is made with hot black coffee and the famous imported Dutch liqueur Vandermint. It combines the flavors of coffee, chocolate and mint.*

Amaretto Coffee *You'll find that the liqueur Amaretto will greatly enhance a cup of hot coffee!*

FIGURE 33 (Cont.)

After Dinner Drinks

A delicious finishing touch to a fine meal!

Velvet Hammer *An old classic with quite a distinctive flavor. It's made with Cointreau, Creme de Cacao and cream.*

Midori and Cream *This delicious cocktail combines the cool, fresh taste of Honeydew Melon and cream.*

Pink Squirrel *The combination of Creme de Noyaux, cream and Creme de Cacao has always been a favorite with the ladies.*

Golden Cadillac *This is one of the all-time favorite after dinner drinks. It's made with Galliano, Creme de Cacao and cream.*

Ice Cream Hopper *The famous Grasshopper can taste even better when made with Vanilla ice cream!*

A fine liqueur by itself can be quite a fulfilling after dinner drink, especially when served in a heated brandy snifter. You'll fine that the aroma and flavor of all liqueurs will be greatly enhanced by the warmth of the snifter.

If you'd like to try a liqueur, may we suggest the distinctively fine tastes of,

Tia Maria *or* **Amaretto**

Grand Marnier

FIGURE 33 (Cont.)

prepared with double shots of liquor while being sold at the regular single shot price. These periods are usually scheduled for the late afternoon on Monday through Friday, to encourage sales to those getting off work at that time, and may last only one hour or, to promote further sales, extend into the early evening.

Because well liquor is usually very inexpensive, implementing a happy hour can be quite a profitable merchandising technique. For example, if well drinks are sold for $1.50 and the average cost per ounce of well liquor is $.14, the average percentage cost of a well drink would be 9.33 percent. Therefore, if double shots are being sold during happy hour at regular drink price the average percentage cost per drink would still be only 18.66 percent, allowing management a sizable gross profit of 81.34 percent.

Special Events

Special events, such as holidays or important sporting events, should always be thought of as opportunities for creative promotions. For example, a costume contest might be considered for Halloween, free hot dogs and popcorn during Monday night football games, complimentary champagne on New Year's Eve, lowered beer prices during the World Series games, or special prices for Irish whiskey on Saint Patrick's day.

Imagination and consistency are again the keys to success. The more creative or unusual the promotion the better the response of the lounge customers.

Hors d'Oeuvres

Providing complimentary hors d'oeuvres in the cocktail lounge is a common practice. As a result, competition in this area of merchandising can be stiff; therefore, to ensure a significant increase in sales, management must put in the time and expense necessary to prepare exceptional hors d'oeuvres.

Because so many bars offer hors d'oeuvres, not only quality but uniqueness will have a bearing on success in this area. Because cooks often consider the preparation of hors d'oeuvres to be a boring, undesirable, and time-consuming chore, it is usually better for management to assign the preparation duties to a single person and then check the results daily.

From the standpoint of cost, hors d'oeuvres will seldom be one of the more profitable merchandising techniques and should not be thought of as such. Besides the high cost of food, there is also the cost of labor to prepare the food and the cost of paper goods, such as napkins and picks.

It is best to consider hors d'oeuvres more as a means of attracting new customers than a means of immediately increasing profits. Certainly imaginative, good tasting hors d'oeuvres will eventually increase sales, but as the customers increase so will the cost of the food and the time involved to prepare it. Quality hors d'oeuvres will, over a period of time, bring new customers to the restaurant, which will eventually result in a general increase in sales during all hours. This is what management must consider when analyzing the importance of hors d'oeuvres, not simply the increase in sales during the hours the hors d'oeuvres are offered.

Entertainment

One of the most expensive means of promoting a bar is through live entertainment. This is not to say that live entertainment should not be considered, because it can result in a dramatic increase in sales, but management should first thoroughly consider all of the costs involved.

1) *The entertainers.* The actual cost of the entertainers will differ considerably from area to area, and will also depend upon whether or not there is a union involved. Generally speaking though, good entertainment is quite expensive and management should be cautious before signing any contracts.

2) *Increased labor cost.* To properly handle a substantial increase in sales, it might be necessary to add another bartender, possibly a bartender's helper, one or two more cocktail servers, and possibly one or two door attendants.

3) *Increased wear on carpets and furnishings.* Because of increased use, the carpet will have to be cleaned on a more regular basis and furnishings will have to be repaired more often.

4) *Increased cost of glassware and paper goods.* A substantial increase in sales normally is accompanied by a proportionately higher usage of paper goods and loss of glassware.

5) *Increased cost of rest room maintenance.* Not only will the cost of rest room supplies increase, but rest room fixtures will normally sustain added abuse.

6) *Increased clean up cost.* There will be added labor cost and an added cost in cleaning supplies involved in cleaning the cocktail lounge each day.

7) *Advertising costs.* If the live entertainment is going to be promoted, advertising costs must be considered.

After these costs have been considered, management should next consider the capacity of the cocktail lounge. Obviously, the potential sales will be limited by the size of the lounge area. Therefore, before projecting potential sales, management should realistically determine the maximum potential.

There are methods by which a sizable portion of these added costs can be recouped, which should also be analyzed. First, the sales price of drinks should be increased at the time the entertainment starts. This is a common practice and should not meet with any customer resistance. Second, a cover charge can be charged at the door. Charging each customer a small cover charge can be extremely profitable, but it will also result in the loss of a percentage of customers. Whether or not this technique should be used depends upon the area, the competition, and the quality of the entertainment.

When calculating the needed sales increase to pay for all the added costs involved, management should remember to subtract the estimated cover charge revenue from the total cost, and calculate the *gross percentage markup* as higher than usual due to the increased prices charged during entertainment periods.

A sample calculation might look as follows:

Gross percentage markup calculation based on five days of entertainment:

Cost of Entertainment	$1,200.00
Secondary Costs (Labor, Supplies, etc.)	635.00
Total:	1,835.00
Less Cover Charges	525.00
Total Cost:	$1,310.00

Gross percentage markup (based on entertainment prices) = 84.65%

$$\text{Needed sales increase} = \frac{1,310.00}{.8465} = \underline{\$1,547.55}$$

Therefore, the restaurant in the example would have to realize an average daily increase in sales of $309.51 to break even. The figures will differ considerably from bar to bar. If management elects to obtain entertainment, more accurate estimates can be projected after only a short period of time.

Chapter 5

TRAINING FOR PROFESSIONAL BARTENDING

Inventory controls, cost controls, and merchandising techniques are all important factors in bar management, but, contrary to popular belief, they are all of only secondary importance. *The most critical factor in bar management is employee management.* Unfortunately, with respect to bartenders, it is within this area that most restaurant managers fail.

The reason is that the majority of restaurant managers, whether they admit it or not, are simply not fully aware of every aspect of professional bartending. Their knowledge usually only consists of a basic understanding of the mechanics of bartending, and that knowledge will seldom achieve the respect of a crew of bartenders.

To be effective, a manager must possess the ability to:

1) Fully train each new bartender.
2) Establish firm rules pertaining to all of the responsibilities of each bartender.
3) Not allow any continual violations of those rules to pass unnoticed.

This will require an *in depth knowledge of professional bartending. Acquiring that knowledge is the starting point from which to learn professional bar management.*

This chapter will deal with giving you that knowledge. It will actually be in the form of a complete professional bartender's training course. The training will include both the physical mechanics of bartending and those principles of etiquette and customer relations employed by the most professional of bartenders. It will touch upon every aspect of bartending that a manager *must* be aware of.

There will be no effort to cover detailed principles of distilling processes or historical aspects of any area of bartending, for these are actually separate fields of study which have very little to do with liquor management.

You'll find that you'll progress through the training much faster and retain much more information if you proceed through the steps in order and take the time to fully understand the principles outlined in each step before moving on.

The final step will be in the form of a test (in the Appendix of this book) that will allow you the opportunity to judge your expertise. A competent bar manager should be able to answer each question *without hesitation*.

GENERAL VOCABULARY

It's far easier to make a study of any new field if you first take the time to familiarize yourself with the associated vocabulary. The words and phrases listed below should be thoroughly understood and memorized.

After Dinner Drink—A dessert drink, often creamy with a liqueur base. A liqueur by itself or with coffee is often ordered as an after dinner drink.

Alphonse—A term indicating a float of cream.

Aperitif—A liqueur, wine, or cocktail taken before a meal to stimulate the taste buds. Dubonnet, Campari, and port wines are all popular aperitifs.

Back—Refers to a second cocktail, liquor, or often, mix being served in a separate glass in "back" of the original request. For example, an order of "vodka rocks with a water back" would be served in two glasses, one with vodka and ice, and the other with ice water.

Back Bar—The bar area located directly behind the bartender, usually used for glass storage and sometimes a liquor display.

Bar Sugar—A finely granulated sugar which dissolves rapidly.

Beer Glass—The glass in which beer is served. The most popular styles are the mug, pilsner, and hour glass. The sizes usually vary from eight to ten ounces.

Bitters—A very concentrated, distinctively bitter mix, which today is used almost exclusively in the preparation of an Old-Fashioned.

Blended Whiskey—A straight whiskey in combination with either another whiskey, neutral spirit, or a combination of both. It's characteristically light in flavor and body.

Bottled in Bond—A federal guarantee that the content of the bottle is straight whiskey, at least four years old, bottled at 100 proof, and the product of a single distillation at a single distillery in a single season.

Contrary to popular belief, this guarantee has nothing to do with the quality of liquor and is used primarily for financial (taxation) reasons.

Bourbon—Whiskey distilled at not more than 160 proof, from a fermented mash of at least 51 percent corn and aged at least two years in new charred oak barrels.

Brandy—Any spirit distilled from fruit.

Brandy Snifter—A short stemmed glass, large and rounded at the bottom and tapering to a small opening at the top to concentrate the aroma. Always used to serve brandy and cognac.

Breakage—An outdated term referring to the emptied bottles at the end of a bartenders shift.

Bucket—An abbreviated name for the Double Old-Fashioned glass.

Build—A method of preparing a cocktail by pouring all the ingredients directly into the glass, as opposed to first using a blender, mixing can, or mixing glass.

Burgundy—One of the great wine regions of France. In most restaurants and bars Burgundy simply means red, and a glass of Burgundy refers to a glass of red wine.

Call Liquor—In bars, any liquor (not liqueur) other than well liquor. The term "call" refers to the customer "calling" for a particular brand as opposed to a type. For example, *Tanqueray* and tonic as opposed to *gin* and tonic.

Canadian Whisky—Whiskey imported from Canada. Generally blended, and very smooth and mellow in nature.

Carafe—A glass or crystal decanter. Sometimes this term is used instead of "liter" when ordering house wines at a restaurant.

Chablis—A dry white wine originating in the Burgundy region of France. In most bars and restaurants Chablis means white and a glass of Chablis is a glass of white wine.

Champagne Glass—A stemmed shallow glass with a normal capacity of four to five ounces.

Chilling—There are generally two ways to chill a glass. The quickest way is to simply bury the glass in crushed ice. The best way is to dip the glass into clean cold water and then refrigerate it.

Cognac—A brandy produced in the Cognac region of France.

Cordial—Synonymous with the term "liqueur," but usually used when referring to the less expensive domestic liqueurs.

Cordial Glass—A small, narrow, stemmed glass used exclusively to serve cordials or liqueurs.

Cocktail Glass—A very broad term often used to describe the type of glass used to serve mixed "up" drinks (cream drinks, Gimlets, Daiquiris, etc.)

Dash—A measurement equivalent to approximately ⅙ tsp.

Dessert Drink—Synonymous with "after-dinner drink," but usually specifically refers to the creamy liqueur-based drinks.

Display Case—A showcase used to display the liquor inventory of the bar.

Double—A type of cocktail in which twice the normal amount of liquor is used.

Double Old-Fashioned Glass—A large bucket-shaped glass usually holding about 12 to 13 ounces.

Draw—Refers to a draft beer. The instruction "draw one" would mean to draw one glass of beer.

Dry—A term which varies with the cocktail. A Dry Martini would mean one using very little dry vermouth, while a Dry Manhattan or Rob Roy would mean using dry vermouth instead of sweet vermouth.

Extra Dry—A term commonly associated with a Martini, meaning extremely little or even no dry vermouth.

Flag—A garnish made by "picking" a red cherry to an orange.

Float—To layer a mix or liquor on top of a completed cocktail. Care must be taken to prevent the floated ingredient from readily mixing with the existing cocktail. This can be done by pouring the float very slowly over the back of a mixing spoon and allowing it to "slip" onto the top of the cocktail.

Frappé—A method of preparing a cocktail in which the liquor, or usually liqueur, is poured over packed crushed ice. The ice is mounded over the rim of the glass as in a snow cone.

Free Pour—A method of preparing cocktails without the use of a measuring glass.

Frozen—A cocktail with an extremely icy, slushy texture—almost too thick to drink.

Garnish—The fruit, straws, and/or stirs added to a cocktail after it's been prepared.

German Pour—A long, narrow, slow pouring spout, normally used for vermouths and mixes.

Gin—A very strong, aromatic liquor distilled from rye and other grains, and flavored with juniper berries.

Grenadine—A very sweet pomegranate or red currant flavored syrup.

Gun—A hand-held dispenser attached to a hose, used to dispense water, carbonated mixes (i.e. cola, lemon-lime soda) and sometimes well liquors.

Highball—Classically, a highball meant a cocktail consisting of only bourbon and a single mix. For example, a "water hi" (or water highball) would be bourbon and water. Today, any single liquor and single mix is often referred to as a highball.

Highball Glass—The glass used for all the basic highball drinks (single liquor + single mix). Usually holds about eight ounces.

House—Refers to the particular restaurant or bar in which the bartender is working. The "house" vodka would be the well vodka and the "house" rules would be the rules of the bar or restaurant.

Hot—A term that comes up most often in reference to a Bloody Mary, it refers to added Tabasco sauce.

Irish Whiskey—A normally blended whiskey imported from Ireland. It derives its unique taste from a triple distillation process and the use of pot stills.

Jigger—A measuring glass used to measure liquor. The size of the glass varies, but ⅞ oz. is the most popular.

Kosher Salt—Large-grained salt used primarily for salting the rim of glasses.

Lime Juice—A heavy, tart, lime flavored syrup.

Lime Squeeze—A wedge of fresh lime used as a garnish.

Lime Wheel—A round slice of fresh lime used as a garnish.

Liter—Equal to 33.8 oz. House wine is often sold by the liter and half liter.

Liqueur—A distinctively flavored, very strong, sweet, syrupy liquor.

Margarita Glass—A large cocktail glass, usually similar in shape to a large wine glass or goblet. Normally about ten ounces in size.

Martini Glass—A tall stemmed glass used to serve Martinis, Manhattans and Rob Roys. Usually about four ounces in size.

Mist—Refers to using crushed ice instead of cubed.

Mixing Can—A steel can used with an electric mixer and strainer. The *mixing can* is used when it's desirable to first blend and then strain the ingredients of a cocktail.

Mixing Glass—A large, thick, heavy glass used with cubed ice, a *mixing spoon*, and strainer to gently mix and chill the ingredients of a cocktail.

Mixing Spoon—A long-handled metal spoon used to stir the ingredients in a *mixing glass*.

Muddler—A wooden stick used to smash or "muddle" cubed sugar or any desired garnish into the bottom of a glass.

On and Over—A method of preparing a cocktail in which the ingredients are first mixed "on" the mixer and then strained "over" cubed ice.

On the Rocks—Over cubed ice.

Orgeat—A very rich almond flavored syrup used extensively in the preparation of tropical cocktails.

Orange Flower Water—A mild, pleasant smelling mix, used almost exclusively in the famous Ramos Fizz.

Over—Means "over" cubed ice.

Par—Refers to the exact number of bottles of a particular type of liquor or wine stored at the bar for backup purposes. For example, if three bottles of Jack Daniel's are stored at the bar, the "par" for Jack Daniel's would be three. Each morning, after the previous night's emptied bottles have been replaced, the entire bar should be at "Par."

P.C.—A commonly used abbreviation for *percentage cost*. It's the percentage of net sales which equals the cost of the inventory used.

Pink Wine—Rosé wine.

Port—A very sweet, fortified wine, often served as an aperitif.

Pouring Spout—For the convenience of the bartender, each opened bottle of liquor is usually capped with a *pouring spout*. These spouts normally come in three speeds, with the fastest having the largest mouth.

Preheat—If a hot drink is to be served in a glass, the glass should always be preheated. A glass can be preheated by filling it and emptying it several times with hot water.

Pre-Mix—Frequently requested cocktails containing a number of ingredients are often *pre-mixed* in quantity ahead of time to aid the efficiency of the bartender.

Premium Call—The most expensive of *call liquors*. Common *premium call* liquors are Chivas Regal, Black Label, Crown Royal, and Wild Turkey.

Proof—Refers to the percentage of alcohol in a liquor. The *proof* is equal to twice the alcoholic percentage. For example, 90 proof bourbon would be 45 percent alcohol.

Quinine—Most commonly referred to as *tonic*. An invigorating, stimulating carbonated mix. Usually a *lime squeeze* is requested when *quinine* is ordered as a mix.

Red Wine—In most bars and restaurants, the term red wine is used interchangeably with Burgundy. It's usually dry and served at room temperature.

Rimming—Refers to coating the lip of a glass with salt or sugar. This is done by first touching the lip of the glass to a sponge saturated with lime juice (if no sponge is available you may run a lime squeeze around the lip of the glass) and then dipping the glass into a bowl of salt or sugar.

Rocks—Cubed ice.

Rock Glass—A short glass (usually four to five ounces) used to serve straight liquor(s) over ice. This glass is used when no mix is requested.

Rosé—A pink wine, served chilled.

Rum—A liquor distilled from the fermented juice of sugar cane, sugar cane syrup, sugar cane molasses, or other sugar cane products.

Rye—Whiskey distilled at not more than 160 proof from a fermented mash of at least 51 percent rye and aged at least two years in new charred oak barrels.

Scotch—A very distinctively flavored, usually blended, whiskey imported from Scotland.

Sherry—A rich amber wine served often as an aperitif. True *sherrys* are always imported from Spain.

Sherry Glass—A small stemmed glass, usually two to three ounces in size. Often used to serve port wine as well as sherry.

Shooter—A slang term used to describe a straight shot.

Shot—Refers to one ounce of liquor served straight.

Simple Syrup—A sweetener made of only sugar and water.

Soda—Carbonated water.

Sour Glass—A tall, stemmed, very narrow glass use exclusively for serving "sours." Normally four to six ounces in size.

Sour Mash—A process of distillation in which the residue from a previous fermentation is added to the new mash to assist continuity of character and reinforce the flavor and bouquet. Jack Daniels is an example of a popular *sour mash* whiskey.

Speed Pour—A pouring spout with a very wide opening or mouth, allowing for a very rapid flow of liquor.

Speed Rack—A rack designed to hold liquor bottles and mixes. It's usually located in the *well area* to give the bartender quick access to popular brands of liquor and often used mixes.

Splash—A unit of measure equal to about a quarter ounce.

Split—A small bottle (usually of champagne) about six to eight ounces in size.

Squeeze—Refers to a lime squeeze, which, when served as a garnish, is squeezed and then dropped into the drink.

Stirred—When a cocktail is ordered "stirred," it's *stirred* in a *mixing glass* before being served.

Straight Whiskey—Whiskey that is not blended with another whiskey or neutral spirit and is stored for at least two years. Usually very pronounced in flavor and character. The most popular *straight whiskeys* are bourbon and rye.

Sweet—Most cocktails are sweetened by simply adding either sugar or simple syrup. Manhattans and Rob Roys are sweetened by adding more sweet vermouth.

Sweet-Sour—A premix commonly used in place of lemon juice and sugar.

Tall—Refers to a drink prepared in a *tall highball* glass. Tall drinks are slightly more diluted due to the extra mix used to fill the glass.

Tall Highball Glass—A tall thin glass, usually two to three ounces larger than a regular highball glass. Sometimes referred to as a *chimney glass*.

Tequila—The national liquor of Mexico, distilled from a fermented mash derived principally from the Agave Tequilana Weber—a type of desert cactus found in Mexico.

Tonic—Synonymous with quinine.

Topless—Refers to "no salt." For example, a topless margarita would be a Margarita without a salt rimmed glass.

Twist—A garnish made from a slice of lemon peel. The peel is "twisted" over the top of the drink before being dropped in.

Up—Refers to serving liquor or a cocktail straight as opposed to over ice.

Virgin—Any cocktail prepared without liquor.

Vodka—A neutral spirit usually distilled from grains (not potatoes, as is commonly thought), which have been filtered through activated carbon to assure that any taste is removed. Vodka has no color, aroma, or taste, and is not aged.

Well Area—The primary work area of the bartender. The ice, well liquor, the majority of the bartender's equipment, and most of the mixes are stored in this area.

Well Liquor—The "house" brands of vodka, bourbon, gin, scotch, rum, brandy, and tequila. If a customer were to order a "vodka and tonic" he would receive the *well vodka*.

Wet—Generally refers to either a more diluted or milder-tasting cocktail. For example, a "wet" martini would be prepared with added vermouth and proportionately less gin. A "wet" scotch and water would be prepared with added water.

Whiskey—An alcoholic distillate from a fermented mash of grain produced at less than 190 proof in such a manner that the distillate possesses the taste, aroma, and characteristics generally attributed to whiskey.

White Wine—In most bars and restaurants, this commonly refers to Chablis. White wines are always served cold and preferably in a chilled glass.

Wine Glass—Usually a stemmed rounded glass about six to eight ounces in size.

TYPES AND BRANDS OF LIQUOR

Although it's not imperative that a bartender have detailed knowledge of the history and distilling processes of each brand of liquor, it is important that he or she have a good understanding of the various categories of liquor and the major brands of each category.

For example, if a bartender is asked, "What is Crown Royal?" the reply, "A blended Canadian whiskey" is enough. It's not important that the bartender realize when it was first introduced or even how it tastes, but he or she should know that it's *Canadian* and that it is a *blended whiskey*.

In reading the material listed in this step, center most of your attention on memorizing the *brands*. It's very important that you learn to associate each brand of liquor with its appropriate category.

Whiskey

Whiskey is defined as a strong alcoholic liquor distilled from the fermented mash of various grains, especially of rye, wheat, corn, or barley. Unfortunately, many brands of liquor fall under this broad definition and as a result there are a number of classifications of whiskey.

Whiskeys are categorized by their nationality and by their ingredients, as listed below.

Nationality

Scotch Whisky
Irish Whiskey
Canadian Whisky

Ingredients

Straight Whiskey
Blended Whiskey
Rye Whiskey
Bourbon Whiskey
Sour Mash Whiskey

Below is a list of the most popular brands of whiskey, categorized first by nationality and then by the nature of their ingredients.

American Whiskey

Straight Bourbon Whiskey

Ancient Age
Early Times
I.W. Harper
Jack Daniels (Sour Mash)
Jim Beam
Old Crow
Old Fitzgerald
Old Forester

Old Grand Dad
Old Taylor
Wild Turkey

Blended Whiskey

Fleischmann's Preferred Blend
Kessler
Schenley Reserve
Seagram's 7 Crown

Rye Whiskey

Old Overholt

Canadian Whisky

Blended Canadian Whisky

Seagram's V.O.
Seagram's Crown Royal
Canadian Club
Black Velvet

Irish Whiskey

Blended Irish Whisky

Murphy's
Old Bushmills
Paddy's
Tullamore Dew

Scotch Whisky

Blended Scotch Whisky

Ballantine's
Black & White
Chivas Regal (12 years old)

Cutty Sark
Dewar's White Label
J & B
Johnnie Walker Black Label (12 years old)
Johnnie Walker Red Label
Passport
White Horse

Gin

England has for a long time been recognized as the home of gin, and today the most popular brands of gin are English imports.

American Gin

Calvert
Fleischmann's
Gilbey's
Gordon's
Schenley

Imported Gin

Beefeater
Bombay
Tanqueray
Plymouth

Vodka

Originally a Russian import, most vodka is now distilled in the United States.

American Vodka

Crown Russe
Fleischmann's
Gilbey's

Gordon's
Kamchatka
Relska
Schenley
Smirnoff
Wolfschmidt

Russian Vodka

Stolichnaya (always stored in the refrigerator)

Polish Vodka

Polmos Polonaise
Polmos Wyborowa Polish

Chinese Vodka

Great Wall Vodka

Rum

Rums are categorized by the area in which they are distilled, and as a result there are at least a dozen varieties of rum. Fortunately, a bartender really need only be concerned with two, Puerto Rican rums (the lightest, most subtle tasting of rums) and Jamaican rums (the strongest, most full bodied rums).

Both Puerto Rican and Jamaican rums are bottled in *light* (sometimes referred to as *silver*) and *dark* (sometimes referred to as *amber* or *gold*) varieties. Generally, the darker the rum the more distinctive its character.

The term 151 rum refers to a 151 proof rum, which is normally golden in color and very harsh in taste.

The most popular brands are as follows:

Puerto Rican Rums

Bacardi (Silver, Amber, and 151)
Ron Rico (White, Gold, and 151)

Jamaican Rum

Myers
Appleton
Lemon Hart

Tequila

Tequila is sold in two shades, *white* and *gold*. *Gold* tequila has been aged in oak vats and has a softer, more full bodied taste.

A few of the most popular brands are:

José Cuervo (White and Gold)
Montezuma (White and Gold)
Pepe Lopez (White and Gold)
Two Fingers (White and Gold)
Puerto Vallarta (White and Gold)

Brandy and Cognac

Brandy is distilled from fruit (as opposed to grain). Cognac is a brandy distilled in the Cognac region of southwestern France. Therefore, all Cognacs are brandy, but not all brandy is Cognac.

Some of the most popular brands of each are:

Brandy

Christian Brothers
E & J
Korbel
Coronet
Paul Masson
Metaxa (Greek Brandy)

Cognac

Courvosier

Hennessy
Martell
Remy Martin

Liqueurs and Cordials

Although the terms "liqueur" and "cordial" are essentially synonymous, *cordial* is usually used when referring to domestic products, while *liqueur* is most often used when speaking of imports.

Liqueurs

Liqueurs are generally the most expensive part of a bar's inventory. The brands listed below are imported from all over the world.

Amaretto—An Italian almond-flavored liqueur made from apricot kernels.

Benedictine—A distinctively flavored liqueur distilled from herbs and brandy. Discovered in 1510 and named after the Benedictine monks.

B&B—Benedictine and brandy

Campari—A sweet wine aperitif liqueur from Italy

Chartreuse—A famous French liqueur still made by a religious order. There are two types, green and yellow, green being much dryer.

Cointreau—A French orange-flavored liqueur.

Drambuie—A scotch-whiskey based liqueur.

Galliano—A golden colored Italian liqueur made from herbs and flowers.

Grand Marnier—A Cognac-based, orange liqueur from France.

Irish Mist—A liqueur produced from Irish whiskey and heather honey.

Kahlua—A Mexican coffee liqueur.

Midori—A honeydew-melon flavored liqueur from Japan.

Ouzo—A Greek, anise-flavored liqueur.

Sambuca—An Italian liqueur made from the Sambuca plant.

Strega—A sweet and spicy Italian liqueur made from herbs and fruits.

Tia Maria—A coffee-flavored liqueur from Jamaica.

Tuaca—An Italian coconut tasting liqueur, known in Italy as "milk brandy."

Vandermint—A chocolate-mint flavored liqueur from Holland.

Cordials

Normally, bars stock only one brand of all of the types of cordials listed below. A few of the most popular brands of cordials are *Arrow, Bols, Dubouchett, Garnier, Leroux* and *Regnier*.

The most popular types of cordials are:

Anisette
Crème de Cacao (Light and Dark)
Crème de Menthe (Green and White)
Crème de Cassis
Crème de Banana
Crème de Noyaux (Almond)
Curaçao (Orange and Blue)
Maraschino
Peppermint Schnapps
Rock & Rye
Sloe Gin
Strawberry Liqueur
Triple Sec
Peach Fruit Liqueur
Blackberry Fruit Liqueur
Apricot Fruit Liqueur

Sherry and Aperitif Wines

Sherry

A true sherry is produced *only* in Spain. Two of the most popular brands of imported sherry are:

Dry Sack
Harvey's Bristol Cream

Many bars will also offer a less expensive domestic sherry. These Sherrys will normally be listed as either:

Cocktail Sherry

Cream Sherry
Dry Sherry
Solera Sherry

Aperitif Wines

The most commonly ordered aperitif wines are:

Dubonnet (always stored in the refrigerator)
Port Wine (Ruby and Tawny)
Vermouth (Sweet and Dry)

THE FUNDAMENTALS OF MIXED DRINKS

Before studying specific recipes, it's important to have a basic understanding of some fundamental concepts pertaining to mixed drinks. General principles associated with methods of preparation, recipes, and glassware are outlined in this section.

Methods of Preparation

Generally, all drinks are prepared by one of the seven methods listed below. Once you fully understand the reasoning behind each method, you'll better understand the reasoning behind the recipes themselves.

Straight Shots

A straight shot means one ounce of liquor served "up." The glassware would be dependent on the type of liquor served.

Liquor—Shot glass
Cordial—Cordial glass
Brandy or Cognac—Snifter
Liqueur—Snifter or Cordial glass

Rock Drinks

A *rock drink* is a straight liquor or combination of liquors (no mix) served over ice. These drinks are served in a *rock glass*, which is normally small because it's designed to serve only liquor(s) without a mix.

Martini rocks, gin rocks, and Black Russians are all examples of *rock drinks*.

Highball Drinks

The basic mixed drink (single liquor + single mix) can be referred to as a *highball drink* and is served in a *highball glass*. The *highball glass* is slightly larger than the *rock glass* to accommodate the added mix. The standard mixes are water, soda, tonic, ginger ale, cola, lemon-lime soda, and fruit juices.

A vodka and tonic, whiskey and water, rum and cola, screwdriver, and greyhound are all examples of *highball drinks* and all should be served in a *highball glass*.

Tall Drinks

Any drink requested "tall" is served in a *tall highball glass*. This glass is slightly larger than a standard *highball glass* to accommodate extra mix. A customer who prefers a milder (more diluted) drink will normally order cocktails tall.

A tall scotch and soda, a tall bourbon and water, and a tall gin and tonic are all examples of tall drinks.

Stirred Drinks

Stirred Drinks are those drinks in which the ingredients are first chilled by being stirred in a *mixing glass*. The ingredients are both chilled and mixed by being stirred with cubed ice. After being stirred, the ingredients are strained into the appropriate glass.

Martinis, Manhattans, and Rob Roys are the most popular of stirred drinks.

Mixing Can Drinks

These drinks are prepared in a steel *mixing can* and are mixed on an electric mixer. The mixer will blend the drinks more thoroughly than the *mixing glass.* The *mixing can* is also used with a strainer to strain the ingredients from the ice.

Most cream drinks are prepared with the *mixing can.*

Blended Drinks

Drinks are prepared in the *blender* when a heavy, thick texture is desired. No strainer is used with the *blender* because the ingredients are actually blended together with the ice to form a "slushy" type of cocktail.

Margaritas and fruit daiquiris are popular *blended drinks.*

Recipes

Unfortunately, there is very little consistency within the liquor industry regarding recipes, and over the years recipes have varied considerably. As a result two bartenders will often prepare the same cocktail quite differently.

The recipes listed on pages 131 through 151 have been proven successful through years of actual use. If you follow them closely you can be confident of the quality of your work, but never be startled to see another bartender prepare a cocktail in a different manner.

Liquor portioning is another area that varies widely, but generally speak‑ ing you'll never be far off if you pour 1¼ oz. for all of your basic drinks (rock drinks, highball drinks and tall drinks), 1 oz. for all of your liqueurs and cordials, and the portions listed on the following pages for all of your mixed and blended drinks.

Glassware

Glassware is still another area of inconsistency. Today, shapes and sizes vary so radically that you're better off memorizing the general types of glassware rather than the styles.

Basically there are about 15 different types of glassware used in most bars. You should recognize the uses of each of the glasses shown in Figure 34. If you've forgotten any, recheck the definitions.

PRIMARY COCKTAILS

It's important to thoroughly study the recipes for the most traditionally

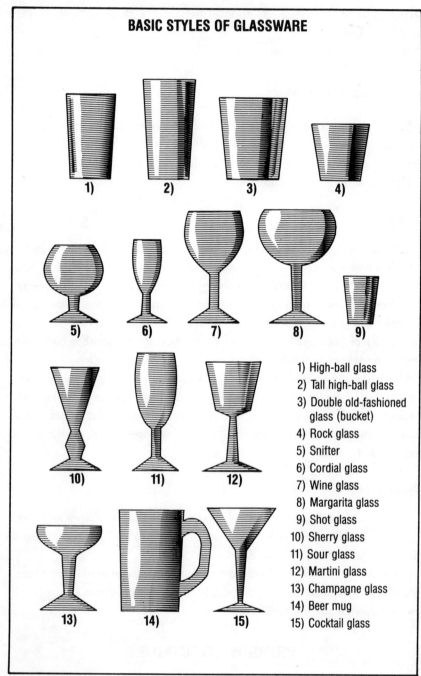

BASIC STYLES OF GLASSWARE

1) High-ball glass
2) Tall high-ball glass
3) Double old-fashioned glass (bucket)
4) Rock glass
5) Snifter
6) Cordial glass
7) Wine glass
8) Margarita glass
9) Shot glass
10) Sherry glass
11) Sour glass
12) Martini glass
13) Champagne glass
14) Beer mug
15) Cocktail glass

FIGURE 34

popular mixed drinks because they represent the great majority of all drinks ordered. The bartender *must* have these drinks memorized to the point of being able to *instantly* recall their ingredients *without hesitation.*

In this section, each recipe will be organized in the following manner:

NAME (Abbreviated Name)
      Glassware—Type of ice
      Method of preparation
          1) Ingredient
          2) Ingredient
          3) Ingredient
      Finishing preparations
GARNISH

Many students have found it easier to memorize the recipes by practicing with flash cards. You can easily make your own set by using blank 3 x 5 cards. On the front of each card print the full name of the cocktail. On the back of the card list, *in order,* the abbreviated name, the glassware, the type of ice, the method of preparation, the ingredients, and finally the garnish. *Memorize all recipes in exactly this order.*

You should also color code your cards with relation to the base liquor. For example, you might write all vodka drinks in blue, all bourbon drinks in black, all gin drinks in red, etc.

Figure 35 is an example of how a flash card should be written.

Bourbon

MANHATTAN (Man)
      Martini glass (chilled)
      Mixing glass + 1 scoop of cubed ice
          1¼ oz. bourbon
          ¾ oz. sweet vermouth
      Stir and strain
RED CHERRY (Stir stick if served on the rocks)

If served on the rocks, the mixing glass would not be used and the drink would simply be built in a rock glass filled with cubed ice.

FLASH CARD

Front

BLACK RUSSIAN

Back

1.) RUSSIAN
2.) ROCK GLASS
3.) CUBED ICE
4.) BUILD
5.) 1¼ oz. VODKA
    ½ oz. KAHLUA
6.) STIR STICK

FIGURE 35

A Manhattan can be made sweeter by using more sweet vermouth and less bourbon.

DRY MANHATTAN (Dry Man)

A Dry Manhattan is prepared in the same manner as a regular Manhattan, with the following two exceptions:

1) Dry vermouth is used in place of sweet vermouth
2) Garnish with an olive in place of a cherry

PERFECT MANHATTAN (Perfect Man)

A Perfect Manhattan is prepared in the same manner as a regular Manhattan, with these two exceptions:

1) Equal portions of sweet vermouth and dry vermouth are used in place of sweet vermouth
2) Garnish with a twist in place of a cherry

OLD-FASHIONED (Fashion)

Rock glass—Cubed ice
Build
   ½ tsp. sugar (sprinkled over the ice)
   3 dashes of bitters (over the sugar)
   1½ oz. bourbon
   Splash of water
Mix all of the ingredients *very well* with a bar spoon
ORANGE, RED CHERRY, TWIST, STIR STICK

Classically this cocktail was prepared by first saturating a cube of sugar with bitters and then, before adding the ice, a muddler was used to grind the cube into the bottom of the glass. A splash of water was added to help dissolve the sugar. Because of the time involved, this method is today seldom used.

PRESBYTERIAN (Press)

Highball glass—Cubed ice
Build
   1¼ oz. bourbon
   Fill remainder of glass half with soda and half with ginger ale
TWIST, STIR STICK

WHISKEY SOUR (Sour)

Sour glass (chilled)

Mixing can + half a scoop of crushed ice

    1¼ oz. bourbon

    3 oz. sweet-sour

Mix for 5 seconds and strain

ORANGE, RED CHERRY, AND TWO SHORT STRAWS

If served on the rocks, the mixer would not be used and the drink would simply be built in a rock glass filled with cubed ice. When served over ice a stir stick is used instead of two short straws.

There are a number of popular "Sours" (scotch sour, rum sour, apricot sour) and they are all prepared in the same manner as a whiskey sour, with only the base liquor being changed.

Gin

MARTINI (Marti)

Martini glass (chilled)

Mixing glass—1 scoop of cubed ice

    2 oz. gin

    Dash of dry vermouth

Stir and strain

OLIVE (Stir stick if on the rocks)

If served on the rocks, the mixing glass would not be used and the drink would be built in a rock glass filled with cubed ice.

A *dry martini* would be prepared with very little dry vermouth.

An *extra dry martini* would be prepared with no dry vermouth.

SINGAPORE SLING (Sling)

Tall glass—crushed ice

Build

    1¼ oz. gin

    2 oz. sweet-sour

    ½ oz. grenadine

    Fill with soda

Mix these ingredients well with a long straw

Float cherry flavored brandy

LIME SQUEEZE, ORANGE, RED CHERRY, TWO LONG STRAWS

TOM COLLINS (Tom)

Tall glass—crushed ice

Build

1¼ oz. gin

Fill remainder of glass half with sweet-sour and half with lemon-lime soda

LIME SQUEEZE, ORANGE, RED CHERRY, TWO LONG STRAWS

Collins mix is always made by mixing together equal amounts of sweet-sour and lemon-lime soda.

There are a number of different Collins drinks, but only the base liquor is different. The glassware, ice, mix, and garnish for all Collins drinks are the same.

The two other most popular collins are the *John Collins* (prepared with bourbon) and the *Vodka Collins* (prepared with vodka).

Scotch

ROB ROY (Rob)

A Rob Roy is prepared in *exactly* the same manner as a Manhattan, except that scotch is used in place of bourbon.

Dry and Perfect Rob Roys are also prepared in exactly the same manner as Dry and Perfect Manhattans, with the base liquor of scotch being the only difference. The portions, methods of preparation, glassware and even garnishes are the same.

It may be helpful to think of Rob Roys as "Scotch Manhattans."

RUSTY NAIL (Nail)

Rock glass—cubed ice

Build

1¼ oz. scotch

½ oz. drambuie

STIR STICK

Vodka

VODKA MARTINI (Vodka Marti)

A Vodka Martini is prepared in *exactly* the same manner as a regular Martini, except that vodka is used in place of gin.

BLACK RUSSIAN (Russian)

Rock glass—cubed ice
Build
      1¼ oz. vodka
      ½ oz. Kahlua
STIR STICK

If you float ¾ oz. of cream on top of a Black Russian you'll have a *White Russian.*

BLOODY MARY (Mary)

Bucket glass (rimmed with salt)—cubed ice
Build
      1¼ oz. vodka
      Dash salt
      Dash celery salt
      ¼ oz. Worcestershire sauce
      ½ oz. beef bouillon
      Dash of Tabasco sauce
      Fill with thick tomato juice
Stir all of the ingredients well
CELERY STICK, LIME SQUEEZE

Because of the number of ingredients involved, most bars use a Bloody Mary mix. With this mix the bartender need only add the vodka.

If you prepare a Bloody Mary with tequila you'll have a *Bloody Maria.*

GREYHOUND (Hound)

Highball glass—cubed ice
Build
      1¼ oz. vodka
      Fill with grapefruit juice
STIR STICK
If the glass is rimmed with salt a Greyhound is called a Salty Dog.

SCREWDRIVER (Driver)

A Screwdriver is prepared in *exactly* the same manner as a Greyhound, except that orange juice is used in place of grapefruit juice.

If you prepare a Tall Screwdriver and float ½ oz. of Galliano on top you'll have a Harvey Wallbanger.

GIMLET

> Cocktail glass (chilled)
> Mixing can + ½ scoop of crushed ice
>> 1¼ oz. vodka
>> 3 oz. lime juice
> Mix for 5 seconds and strain
> GREEN CHERRY, LIME WHEEL, 2 SHORT STRAWS (Stir stick if on the rocks)

Traditionally, a Gimlet has always been made with gin, but within recent years vodka has become the more commonly used base.

Some people will enjoy a splash of sweet-sour in their Gimlet to reduce the tartness of the lime juice.

If served on the rocks, the mixing can would not be needed and the drink would be built in a rock glass filled with cubed ice.

Tequila

MARGARITA (Maggie)

> Margarita glass (rimmed with salt)
> Blender + 2 scoops of crushed ice
>> 1¼ oz. tequila
>> ½ oz. Triple Sec
>> 3 oz. Margarita mix
> Blend for 10 seconds and pour
> LIME WHEEL, TWO SHORT STRAWS

Most bars will either prepare their own, or buy a bottled Margarita mix. If no mix is available, you can use straight sweet-sour with a splash of orange juice and ½ oz. of lime juice as a substitute.

If you add 2 oz. of strawberries and a little less Margarita mix you'll create a *Strawberry Margarita*. Strawberry Margaritas should be rimmed with sugar instead of salt.

TEQUILA SUNRISE (Sunrise)

> Tall highball glass—crushed ice
> Build
> > ¾ oz. grenadine
>
> Fill the glass with crushed ice *after* pouring the grenadine into the bottom of the empty glass. Then pour
> > 1¼ oz. tequila
> > Fill remainder of glass with orange juice
>
> Make the grenadine rise about half way up the glass by mixing the bottom of the glass with 2 long straws
> > Float ¼ oz. creme de cassis
>
> LIME SQUEEZE, RED CHERRY, ORANGE, TWO LONG STRAWS

This can be quite a beautiful cocktail if you take the necessary time to build it in the exact manner listed in this recipe. The bottom of the glass should be deep red in color while the top should remain bright orange.

Rum

DAIQUIRI

> Cocktail glass (chilled)
> Mixing can + ½ scoop of crushed ice
> > 1¼ oz. rum
> > 2 oz. sweet-sour
> > 1 tsp. sugar
>
> Mix for 5 seconds and strain
> TWO SHORT STRAWS (Stir stick if on the rocks)

If you substitute ½ oz. grenadine for the sugar and use Bacardi Rum you'll have a *Bacardi Cocktail.*

MAI TAI

> Bucket glass—¼ full of cubed ice
> Mixing can + 1 scoop of crushed ice
> > 1 oz. light rum
> > 1 oz. dark rum

½ oz. orange curaçao

2 oz. pineapple juice

¾ oz. lime juice

½ oz. orgeat syrup

SPLASH orange juice

Mix and pour (do not strain) over the cubed ice

Pour 2 circles of grenadine around the rim of the glass (approx. ½ oz.)

FLOAT ¾ oz. Jamaican Rum

PINEAPPLE SPEAR, RED CHERRY, TWO LONG STRAWS

The great majority of bars use a bottled Mai Tai mix. With such a mix you need only add the rums and grenadine.

PINA COLADA (Colada)

Tall highball glass

Blender—1½ scoops of crushed ice

1¼ oz. rum

2 oz. coconut cream

2 oz. pineapple juice

SPLASH orange juice

½ oz. cream

Blend for 10 seconds and pour

PINEAPPLE SPEAR, RED CHERRY, TWO LONG STRAWS

Most bars will use a bottled Pina Colada mix, to which you need only add the rum. If you prepare a Pina Colada with vodka instead of rum, you'll create a *Chi Chi*.

FRUIT DAIQUIRIS

Large cocktail glass

Blender—2 scoops of crushed ice

1¼ oz. rum

2 oz. sweet-sour

3 oz. desired fruit

Blend for 10 seconds and pour

FRESH FRUIT, 2 LONG STRAWS

If the fruit is fresh, or frozen but not presweetened, add 2 tsp. of sugar.

The most commonly ordered fruit daiquiris are strawberry, peach, and banana. Most bars will use frozen, presweetened fruit for their strawberry and peach daiquiris and fresh banana for their banana daiquiris.

Brandy

STINGER
    Cocktail glass (chilled)
    Mixing can + ½ scoop of crushed ice
        1 oz. brandy
        ¾ oz. white crème de menthe
    Mix for 5 seconds and strain
    TWO SHORT STRAWS (Stir stick if on the rocks)

If served on the rocks, a Stinger should still be mixed and strained over the ice.

BRANDY ALEXANDER (Alexander)
    Cocktail glass (chilled)
    Mixing can + ½ scoop of crushed ice
        1 oz. brandy
        ¾ oz. dark crème de cacao
    Mix for 5 seconds and strain
    NUTMEG, TWO SHORT STRAWS

SECONDARY COCKTAILS

You'll also need to study the recipes for the remaining cocktails that a bartender should know—cocktails that are still commonly ordered, but not nearly as often as those listed as primary cocktails.

It would be a good idea to also make flash cards for these cocktails and have them color coded in exactly the same manner as the cards listing the primary cocktails.

When finished, you should have two separate stacks of flash cards—*primary cocktails* and *secondary cocktails.*

When studying this step, notice how many cocktails are derived directly from one of the primary cocktails. Keeping this thought in mind will help you memorize many of these less commonly ordered drinks.

You should note any similarities to a primary cocktail on the back of your flash cards. For example, on the back of your Salty Dog card you should write "A *Greyhound* with a salt rimmed glass."

Bourbon

BOILERMAKER

A straight shot of bourbon with a beer "back."

GODFATHER

Rock glass—cubed ice
Build
1¼ oz. bourbon
½ oz. amaretto
STIR STICK

A Godfather may also be made with scotch instead of bourbon. Therefore, always ask the customer how he or she would like the drink prepared.

JOHN COLLINS

A *Tom Collins* prepared with bourbon instead of gin.

SEVEN AND SEVEN (7/7)

Highball glass—cubed ice
Build
1¼ oz. Seagram's 7 Crown
Fill remainder of glass with 7Up
STIR STICK

SNOW SHOE

Rock glass—cubed ice
Build
1¼ oz. Wild Turkey bourbon
¾ oz. peppermint schnapps
STIR STICK

Gin

GIN AND TONIC (G T)

A very common highball drink. Whenever a customer orders tonic, always ask if he or she would care for a lime squeeze.

GIN GIMLET

A *Vodka Gimlet* prepared with gin instead of vodka.

GIN FIZZ

Cocktail glass (chilled)
Mixing can + ½ scoop of crushed ice
  1¼ oz. gin
  3 oz. sweet-sour
  SPLASH of soda
Mix for 5 seconds and strain
RED CHERRY, TWO SHORT STRAWS

PINK LADY

Cocktail glass (chilled)
Mixing can + ½ scoop of crushed ice
  1¼ oz. gin
  ¾ oz. cream
  ½ oz. grenadine
Mix for 5 seconds and strain
TWO SHORT STRAWS

RAMOS FIZZ

Tall highball glass—½ full of cubed ice
Mixing can + ½ scoop of crushed ice
  1¼ oz. gin
  ½ oz. sweet-sour
  1½ tsp. sugar
  2 oz. cream
  The WHITE of a medium-sized egg
Mix for 5 seconds and strain over the cubed ice. Fill the glass ⅘ full and top with soda
  FLOAT 5 drops of Orange Flower Water
TWO LONG STRAWS

SILVER FIZZ
A *Ramos Fizz* without the orange flower water.

ROYAL FIZZ
A *Ramos Fizz* using the whole egg.

GOLDEN FIZZ
A *Ramos Fizz* using only the yolk of the egg.

Scotch

SCOTCH AND SODA (Scottie)
A very common highball drink. Remember the nickname.

GODFATHER
See *Godfather* under "bourbon."

Vodka

BLOODY BULL
Bucket glass (rimmed with salt)—cubed ice
Build
1¼ oz. vodka
Fill glass ¾ full with beef bouillon
Fill remainder of glass with Bloody Mary mix
CELERY STICK, LIME SQUEEZE

BULL SHOT
Bucket glass—cubed ice
Build
1¼ oz. vodka
Fill remainder of glass with beef bouillon
STIR STICK (lime squeeze optional—ask customer)

HARVEY WALLBANGER (Wallbanger)
A *Tall Screwdriver* topped with a ½ oz. float of Galliano.

SALTY DOG
A *Greyhound* with the lip of the glass rimmed with salt.

WHITE RUSSIAN

A *Black Russian* with a ¾ oz. float of cream.

Tequila

BLOODY MARIA

A *Bloody Mary* prepared with tequila instead of vodka.

BRAVE BULL

A *Black Russian* prepared with tequila instead of vodka.

PANTHER

Rock glass—cubed ice
Build
    1½ oz. Tequila
    ½ oz. sweet-sour
STIR STICK

Rum

BACARDI COCKTAIL

A *Daiquiri* that is prepared by substituting grenadine for sugar and using Bacardi Rum.

CHI CHI

A *Pina Colada* prepared with vodka instead of rum.

CUBA LIBRE

A *Rum and Cola* garnished with a lime squeeze.

PLANTER'S PUNCH

Bucket glass—cubed ice
Mixing can + ½ scoop of crushed ice
    1½ oz. dark Jamaican rum
    2 oz. pineapple juice
    2 oz. sweet-sour

½ oz. grenadine

½ oz. lime juice

Mix for 5 seconds and strain over the crushed ice

PINEAPPLE SPEAR, RED CHERRY, TWO LONG STRAWS

NAVY GROG

Bucket glass—crushed ice

Mixing can + ½ scoop of crushed ice

1 oz. dark rum

½ oz. light rum

2 oz. orange juice

2 oz. pineapple juice

½ oz. lime juice

DASH of orgeat syrup

Mix for 5 seconds and strain over the crushed ice

PINEAPPLE SPEAR, RED CHERRY, TWO LONG STRAWS

STRAWBERRY COLADA

A *Pina Colada* prepared with 2 oz. strawberries.

ZOMBIE

Tall highball glass—crushed ice

Build

¾ oz. light rum

¾ oz. dark rum

1 oz. orange juice

½ oz. lime juice

¾ sweet-sour

½ oz. grenadine

FLOAT ½ oz. 151 rum

ORANGE SLICE, RED CHERRY, TWO LONG STRAWS

Brandy

DIRTY MUDDER (Dirty Mother)

A *Black Russian* prepared with brandy instead of vodka.

DIRTY WHITE MUDDER (Separator)

A *Dirty Mudder* with a ¾ oz. float of cream.

SIDE CAR

Cocktail glass (rimmed with sugar)

Mixing can + ½ scoop of crushed ice

1¼ oz. brandy

½ oz. Triple Sec

3 oz. sweet-sour

Mix for 5 seconds and strain

LIME WHEEL, TWO SHORT STRAWS

Liqueurs

GOLDEN CADILLAC (Cadillac)

Cocktail glass

Mixing can + ½ scoop of crushed ice

1 oz. Galliano

¾ oz. light crème de cacao

2 oz. cream

Mix for 5 seconds and strain

TWO SHORT STRAWS

GOLDEN DREAM

Cocktail glass

Mixing can + ½ scoop of crushed ice

1 oz. Galliano

½ oz. Cointreau (or Triple Sec)

¾ oz. orange juice

1½ oz. cream

Mix for 5 seconds and strain

TWO SHORT STRAWS

GRASSHOPPER (Hopper)

Cocktail glass

Mixing can + ½ scoop of crushed ice

¾ oz. green crème de menthe

1 oz. white crème de cacao

2 oz. cream

Mix for 5 seconds and strain

TWO SHORT STRAWS

INTERNATIONAL STINGER

Rock glass—cubed ice

Build

1¼ oz. Metaxa

¾ oz. Galliano

TWIST, TWO SHORT STRAWS

KING ALPHONSE

Cordial glass

Build

Fill glass ⁹⁄₁₀ full with dark crème de cacao

Float cream

Pour the cream very slowly so it layers on top of the dark crème de cacao.

NO GARNISH (If served on the rocks, serve with a stir)

PINK SQUIRREL

Cocktail glass

Mixing can—½ scoop of crushed ice

1 oz. crème de noyaux

1 oz. white crème de cacao

1¾ oz. cream

Mix for 5 seconds and strain

TWO SHORT STRAWS

ROOTBEER FLOAT

Tall highball glass (or beer mug)—cubed ice

Build

1 oz. dark crème de cacao

¼ oz. Galliano

Fill glass ¾ full with cola

Fill remainder of glass with cream

Stir all of the ingredients well with a mixing spoon
Top with whipped cream
RED CHERRY, TWO LONG STRAWS

SLOE GIN FIZZ

A *Gin Fizz* prepared with sloe gin instead of gin.

SMITH AND KERNS

Tall highball glass—cubed ice
Build

1½ oz. dark crème de cacao
2 oz. cream
Fill remainder of glass with soda

ONE LONG STRAW

SMITH AND WESSON

A *Smith and Kerns* prepared with Kahlua instead of dark crème de cacao.

VELVET HAMMER

Cocktail glass
Mixing can + ½ scoop crushed ice

1 oz. Cointreau
¾ oz. dark crème de cacao
2 oz. cream

Mix for 5 seconds and strain
TWO SHORT STRAWS

BANSHEE

Cocktail glass
Mixing can + crushed ice

1 oz. crème de banana
¾ oz. white crème de cacao
2 oz. cream

Mix for 5 seconds and strain
TWO SHORT STRAWS

Coffee drinks

All coffee drinks should be prepared with fresh hot black coffee and served in a bar mug. If they are to be served in a glass mug, the glass should always be preheated.

Unless otherwise specified, all of the drinks listed below should be prepared with four ounces of coffee, topped with a mound of whipped cream, and garnished with a red cherry and two short straws.

CALYPSO COFFEE
    ¾ oz. rum
    ½ oz. Tia Maria

DUTCH COFFEE
    1¼ oz. Vandermint

FUZZY DICK
    ¾ oz. Grand Marnier
    ½ oz. Kahlua

IRISH COFFEE
    1¼ oz. Irish Whiskey
    1 tsp. sugar
    GARNISH with a green cherry

KEOKE COFFEE
    ¾ oz. brandy
    ½ oz. Kahlua
    ¼ oz. dark crème de cacao

MEXICAN COFFEE
    ¾ oz. tequila
    ½ oz. Kahlua
    GARNISH with one red and one green cherry

Wine and Champagne

WINE COOLER
    Tall highball glass—cubed ice
    Build
        Fill glass ¾ full with red wine
        Fill remainder of glass with soda

ONE LONG STRAW

Many prefer rosé instead of burgundy, and some prefer lemon-lime soda instead of club soda. Always ask your customers how they prefer their wine coolers.

SPRITZER
    A *wine cooler* made with white wine and soda and garnished with a twist.

CHAMPAGNE COCKTAIL
    Champagne glass (chilled)
        Place one cube of sugar in the glass and saturate it with 3 dashes of bitters
        Fill the glass with champagne
TWIST

Normally a split of champagne is served with a champagne cocktail.

DUBONNET COCKTAIL
    Martini glass (chilled)
    Mixing glass + 1 scoop of cubed ice
        1¼ oz. gin
        ¾ oz. Dubonnet
    Stir and strain
TWIST

Hot Drinks

HOT BUTTERED RUM

> Bar mug
> Build
>> 1½ oz. rum
>> ¾ tsp. sugar
>> Fill with boiling water
>> Float 1 pad of butter

SPRINKLE NUTMEG, CINNAMON STICK, STIR STICK

HOT TODDY

> Bar mug
> Build
>> 1½ oz. whiskey
>> Fill with boiling water
>> ½ tsp. sugar
>> ½ tsp. cinnamon

CINNAMON STICK, STIR STICK

GARNISHES

No cocktail is complete until it has been fully garnished. This includes the proper fruit, the proper method of serving the fruit, and the proper straw(s) or stir stick. Too many bartenders fail to realize that garnishes can dramatically affect the taste of a cocktail as well as the appearance.

Below is an outline of how each garnish should be *prepared, served,* and *stored.*

Red and Green Cherries

When used in a **flag** (picked to an orange or pineapple), or when used on top of whipped cream, the stem of a cherry should always be removed. When dropped into a mixed drink (i.e. Manhattan) the stem can remain or it can be removed and the cherry picked.

Whether cherries are stored in their original jar or in a garnish tray on the bar, they should always be **submerged** in their own juice to prevent them from drying out.

Green Olives and Onions

Olives and onions should always be served with a **pick.**

As with cherries, olives and onions should always be stored **submerged** in their own juice to keep them fresh.

Lime Squeezes

Lime squeezes are carved as follows:

1) Trim the stem off both ends of the lime.
2) Cut the lime lengthwise into two equal halves.
3) Cut each half lengthwise into three separate wedges.

Larger limes will yield up to ten wedges, while smaller limes will yield only four.

A lime squeeze is served by first squeezing the juice of the lime into the drink and then dropping the entire wedge into the glass. No pick is required with a lime squeeze.

Always store limes in a sealed container in the refrigerator. They will tend to discolor after two days and should be discarded.

Lime Wheels

Lime wheels are carved as follows:

1) Cut at least ¼ inch off the end of the lime to fully expose the meat of the fruit.
2) Starting at one end, proceed to slice the lime into a series of wheels or circles, each being at least ¼ inch thick.
3) Slice a ½ inch notch through the skin, cutting toward the center of each wheel.

A lime wheel is served by sliding the wheel onto the lip of the glass through the ½ inch notch.

Lime wheels should be stored in the same manner as lime wedges, but should be served in the same day they are cut. They tend to wilt and discolor very rapidly.

Lemon Twists

Lemon twists are carved as follows:

1) Always select a large lemon with a thick peel.
2) Cut at least ½ inch off each end of the lemon to fully expose the meat of the fruit.

Before you can cut twists, you must separate the core, or meat, of the lemon from the peel. This requires skill that may take practice. Follow the remaining steps carefully.

3) With a spoon or ice pick, make a small groove around the meat of the lemon. This groove should be between the meat and skin of the lemon.
4) Continue to follow the path of the groove as you slowly start to push the ice pick or spoon deeper and deeper into the lemon. As you push inward you'll be separating the peel from the core of the lemon. Be careful to push slightly outward to avoid cutting into the meat of the fruit.
5) After you've cut through half of the lemon, stop and duplicate the procedure on the opposite end. Eventually, you should be able to push the core of the lemon through the peel.
6) The final step is simply to slice the peel lengthwise into a series of strips about ¼ inch thick.

To serve a lemon twist, hold the twist over the top of the cocktail with the skin facing downward. Then, while holding the ends of the twist between the thumb and forefinger of each hand, twist the ends in opposite directions. This will cause the peel to shoot a faint spray of juices into the cocktail. It will also leave the peel very oily. Finish by rubbing the oily **skin** around the lip of the glass and dropping the entire twist into the cocktail.

Twists should also be stored in a sealed container in the refrigerator. When exposed to air, twists tend to dry out very quickly. Even in the refrigerator, after two days twists will discolor and turn very slimy. Twists are far better, as are most garnishes, if they are used the same day they are cut.

Oranges

Oranges are cut in a manner very similar to **lime wheels,** except that oranges are served as half wheels. After cutting the orange into a series of wheels, cut each wheel in half and then slice from the center of each half wheel outward toward the peel, being careful not to cut through the peel.

Oranges are served by pushing the center of the orange (the notched area) on to the lip of the glass. Half of the orange will be in the drink and half will be on the outside of the glass.

Oranges should always be served on the same day they are cut, otherwise they tend to lose their fresh appearance.

Celery

Use only fresh, very firm stalks of celery. Clean the celery thoroughly before cutting and use only the thickest, greenest stalks of each head. Actually cutting the celery is very simple—just cut each stalk into sticks approximately 5 inches long and a half inch wide.

Celery sticks are served by simply dipping the stick into the drink. The stick is used as a stir as well as an appetizer.

The key to storing celery is to always keep the sticks **submerged** under ice cold water. Under these conditions, the celery will stay firm and crisp for several days.

Pineapple Spears

Always select a very firm pineapple and carve it as follows:

1) Trim off at least an inch and a half off the top of the pineapple.
2) Slice off a wheel about ¾ inch thick.
3) Cut the wheel like a pie, into eight separate wedges.
4) Turn each wedge onto its side and cut a half inch deep groove parallel to the skin. The groove should be about ¼ inch down from the skin.

Mount each wedge by sliding the groove onto the lip of the glass. The wedge should be pointing inward.

Pineapple should only be served the day it is cut. Throughout the day it should be stored in a sealed container in the refrigerator.

Stirs and Straws

Keep the following thoughts in mind about **stirs** and **straws.**

1) Any drink served with ice (**rock drink** or **highball**) should be served with a **stir.** This will allow the customer to further chill the cocktail by stirring the ice.
2) When two short straws are served, they should be balanced horizontally across the top of the glass.
3) **Tall drinks** should be served with one long straw, which the customer can use as a stir.
4) Each time a new drink is served, it should be served with a new **stir,** as well as a new **napkin.**

Generally, the garnishes are primarily the **day bartender's** responsibility. Each morning, before his or her shift, the day bartender should follow these steps:

1) Remove all the garnishes stored in the refrigerator and discard all but the fresh.
2) All the garnish containers should be cleaned.
3) Enough garnishes should be cut to last throughout the day.
4) Any new garnishes cut should be stored behind the old garnishes. (This rotating process is very important with all food items, especially cream and fruit juices.)

TOOLS OF THE TRADE

All bartenders should have a good understanding of the tools and equipment commonly used in the preparation of mixed drinks. The proper methods of using a **jigger, mixing glass, mixing can,** and **blender** are important and should be studied.

The Jigger

Because expert bartenders realize the importance of accurately measuring all liquors, they've learned to become very proficient with the use of a **jigger.**

The jigger is a special measuring glass which was specifically designed to allow the bartender to pour rapidly as well as accurately. It usually stands about three inches tall and is narrow with a heavy base. It comes in a wide variety of sizes with ⅞ oz. being the most popular.

Using a jigger properly looks far easier than it actually is. The only way to really learn the proper method is to continually practice the four steps listed below. You'll need to purchase a jigger and a slow pouring spout (usually the plastic pours sold in liquor stores are relatively slow). You'll also need an empty quart bottle, which you can fill with water.

Four Steps in Using a Jigger

1) With the thumb and forefinger of your left hand, hold the jigger straight up and very close to the left side of the glass. The top of the jigger should be even with the top of the glass.

2) Holding the neck of the bottle with the right hand, start pouring water into the jigger. You should almost completely invert the bottle so that the bottom end of the bottle is raised high in the air to force the water rapidly out of the pouring spout and *straight down* into the jigger. The end of the pour should be very close to the top of the jigger to prevent splashing.

3) Once the jigger has become three quarters full, *in one motion* move the bottle laterally to the right side of the glass with your right hand while pouring the contents of the jigger into the glass with your left hand. While doing this, do not drop the bottom end of the bottle. Keep the water flowing out at the same rate of speed, simply move the bottle laterally to your right. When this motion is completed the jigger should be completely inverted over the top of the glass.

4) After the jigger is empty, cut off the flow of water by rapidly dropping the bottom of the bottle downward. To prevent dripping, you should twist the pour toward you while returning the bottle to its upright position.

Practice these four steps continually until you can consistently pour 30 to 32 shots from a quart bottle. After that, practice pouring 1¼ oz. measures until you can consistently pour 23 to 25 shots from the bottle.

When you practice, always practice at a brisk pace. The entire pouring motion should take only a few seconds.

Pouring Two or More Shots

You must also practice pouring three or four drinks at the same time. For example, if you were going to prepare three vodka and tonics, you wouldn't want to pick up and replace the jigger three separate times to pour three shots of vodka. You would pour all three shots of vodka at the same time by following these four steps:

1) Line up the three glasses very close together.
2) Pour the first shot in the same manner you would if you were preparing only one drink.
3) After you've emptied the jigger, *do not drop the bottle.* Instead, very quickly reverse the jigger under the flow of water and while the jigger is filling for the second time *move both the jigger and bottle* (as if one unit) *over the second glass.*
4) After the jigger is three quarters full, empty it into the second glass. Then repeat Step 3 for the third drink.

When you're practicing preparing three or four drinks at the same time, you must remember to *never cut off the flow of water until you're completely done.* Simply move the inverted bottle across the top of the glasses with your right hand while your left hand and jigger do all of the work. With this motion you'll need to keep the pour higher above the glasses than you would with a single drink, because you'll need extra room to maneuver the jigger under the bottle.

Pouring Doubles

You'll also need to practice pouring doubles (two shots into the same glass). This is done by simply repeating your basic motion twice *without cutting off the flow of water.* After you've completed the first shot, quickly return the jigger to its original position (upright and outside the left side of the glass), and move the bottle laterally back to your left to start refilling the jigger for the second shot.

Measuring Liqueurs and Cordials

Liqueurs and cordials are best measured with a lined shot glass instead of a jigger. Because of this, many bartenders use two measuring glasses, a jigger for liquor and a lined shot glass for the liqueurs and cordials.

Using a jigger properly takes *much practice*. A bartender should spend hours practicing the motions outlined in this step. Studying the diagrams in Figure 36 while practicing will help give a clear picture of the proper movements. Practice *speed, neatness,* and *accuracy.*

The Mixing Glass

The **mixing glass** is a large, thick-walled glass about 20 oz. in size. It's used in conjunction with a **mixing spoon,** cubed ice, and a **mixing glass strainer.**

The mixing glass is used for two reasons:

1) *To chill the ingredients* of a cocktail with a minimal amount of dilution.
2) *To mix the ingredients* of a cocktail without giving the cocktail a cloudy appearance.

Using a mixing glass properly involves only the following four steps:

1) *Fill half the mixing glass with cubed ice.*
   It's best to used only fresh, very cold cubed ice. Never reuse the same ice twice because it will result in too much dilution. Never use crushed ice because it also allows for too much dilution and is sometimes difficult to strain.
2) *Measure and add the desired ingredients.*
   Simply pour the ingredients into the glass over the cubed ice.
3) *Stir the ice with a mixing spoon to mix and chill the ingredients.*
   Always stir the ice at least 15 times to insure the proper degree of chilling and mixing. If you use the proper ice you'll not have to worry about any excessive diluting of the cocktail by stirring it this much.

THE FOUR STEPS TO USING A JIGGER

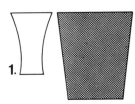

Step One. Notice that the jigger is *very close* and even with the top left-hand side of the glass.

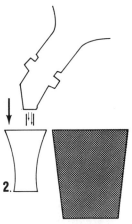

Step Two. Notice that the bottle is raised so high that the liquor is running straight down into the jigger. Also notice that the pour is very close to the top of the jigger.

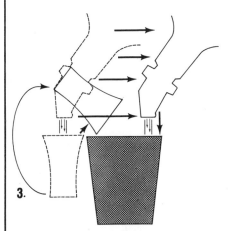

Step Three. The arrows illustrate the lateral movement of the bottle. It's important that both the bottle and jigger are moving at the same time. It's also important that both the jigger and pour stay very close to the top of the glass.

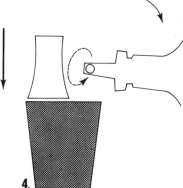

Step Four. While the butt of the bottle is dropping rapidly downward, notice how the pour is turning inward to prevent dripping. The jigger is completely inverted. The jigger and pour stay directly over the top of the glass.

FIGURE 36

Never stir the ice with the handle of the mixing spoon. This commonly practiced procedure is in very poor taste.

4) *Place the strainer over the top of the mixing glass and strain the ingredients into the appropriate class.*

Never let the ingredients sit in the glass very long after stirring. Try to strain the ingredients immediately to prevent unnecessary dilution.

Always check the cleanliness of the strainer before using.

The strainer should be held down firmly with the right forefinger while the mixing glass is inversed and the liquor is strained from the ice. The mixing glass and strainer should be held only in the right hand.

After completing the cocktail, clean and rinse the **mixing glass, mixing spoon,** and **strainer.** Then return them together to their proper place.

The Mixing Can

The **mixing can** is a steel container about the same size as the **mixing glass.** It's used in conjunction with an **electric mixer,** crushed ice and a **mixing can strainer.**

The mixing can mixes and chills the ingredients more thoroughly than a mixing glass, but also tends to dilute the cocktail to a greater degree.

Using the mixing can properly involves only the following four steps:

1) *Fill the can one quarter full of crushed ice.*

Use only fresh, very cold crushed ice. Cubed ice neither mixes nor chills the ingredients as well as crushed ice.

2) *Measure and add the ingredients.*

Simply pour the ingredients into the can and over the crushed ice.

3) *Attach the can to the mixer and mix the ingredients.*

As a general rule of thumb, only use the mixer on the slow speed and never mix the ingredients longer than six to eight seconds. Higher speeds and longer periods of mixing only tend to add to the dilution.

4) *Remove the can from the mixer, place the strainer over the top of the can and strain the ingredients into the appropriate glass.*

Strain the ingredients immediately after removing the can from the mixer.

Always check the cleanliness of the strainer before using.

The strainer should be held firmly down with the right forefinger while the can is inverted and the ingredients are strained from the ice. The mixing can and strainer should be held in only the right hand.

After using the mixing can, clean and rinse the **can, arm of the electric mixer** and the **mixing can strainer.** Then return the can and the strainer to their proper places.

The Blender

Because the blender actually blends the crushed ice and ingredients of the cocktail together, it's used only when a heavy-textured cocktail is desired. No strainer is used with the blender.

Using the blender properly involves the following four steps:

1) *Add the desired amount of crushed ice to the blender.*

Use only crushed ice in the blender, because cubed ice takes far too long to break down and leaves a rough, lumpy drink.

The thickness of the cocktail is directly dependent on the ratio of crushed ice to liquid ingredients. The more crushed ice used, the thicker the resulting cocktail.

2) *Measure and add the desired ingredients.*

Simply pour the ingredients into the blending container over the crushed ice.

3) *Attach the container to the base, cover it with its lid, and blend the ingredients.*

The longer the ingredients are blended, the smoother the resulting texture will be. Therefore, all cocktails should be blended at least 15 seconds.

When preparing **frozen cocktails** (e.g., FROZEN DAIQUIRIS) you'll need to use an excessive amount of crushed ice, and as a result you might have trouble getting the ice to blend. To solve this problem, you'll need to continually stop the blender (wait for the blades to *stop turning)* and, push the crushed ice down onto the blending blades using a mixing spoon.

4) *Turn off the blender and pour the ingredients into the appropriate glass.*

With **frozen drinks** you'll need to use your mixing spoon to help scoop the mixture into the glass.

After using the blender, clean and rinse the blending container and lid.

SPEED AND EFFICIENCY

A bartender can dramatically increase his or her speed by learning to minimize movements by better organizing.

Most new bartenders are slow because they primarily use only one hand. If a bartender is right handed, he or she can learn to use the bar gun (mix dispenser) and pour all of the mixes with the left hand. The right hand then can be used only for pouring liquor, the mixing can, the mixing glass, and the blender. By learning to effectively use both hands, a bartender can greatly reduce preparation time.

Movements can only be minimized by organizing and developing a consistent *routine*. Regardless of how many cocktails the bartender is preparing, they should always be prepared as follows:

1) *Place all of the glassware on the pouring mat.*

Organize the glasses from the shortest to the tallest (left to right). If you're preparing mixed or blended drinks place the mixing glass, mixing can, or blending container on the mat too.

2) *Fill all of the glassware with ice.*

If you're using the mixer or blender, fill them with ice too. Once you've *picked up* the ice scoop don't put it down until you're *completely* through using it and all of the ice (cubed and crushed) has been scooped.

3) *Measure and pour all of the liquor.*

Once you pick up the jigger, don't put it down until all of the liquor has been poured.

4) *Add the remaining ingredients to the mixer or blender.*

It saves time to have the mixer and blender working while you finish preparing the remaining cocktails.

5) *With your left hand, add the final mixes.*
6) *With your right hand, pour the mixed and blended drinks and you should be finished.*

A fast, efficient bartender must develop a routine similar to this and make that routine *habitual*. Whether the bar is very busy or extremely slow, all drinks should be prepared in exactly the same manner.

It's very important that when preparing a group of cocktails that the bartender learn to pick up the ice scoop, bar "gun," jigger, each mix, and each liquor *only once*. For example, instead of measuring the liquor for just one drink, once picking up the jigger the bartender can measure and pour the liquor for all the drinks. Picking up and replacing the jigger five times to prepare five cocktails, wastes much time.

Whether preparing two drinks or ten drinks, the bartender must make a conscious effort to prepare all of the drinks at once and *never one at a time*.

With regards to speed, there are only two rules that must be remembered:

1) You must learn to be proficient with *both hands*.
2) You must develop a *consistent routine*.

THE ART OF BARMANSHIP

The complete bartender must master all of the aspects of *barmanship*. In other words, he or she must not only possess all of the mechanical skills of bartending, but must also have a good understanding of *human relations* and a thorough knowledge of proper *bar etiquette*.

The key points of the very important areas of *human relations* and *bar etiquette* must be studied.

Human Relations

Customer rapport is a critical part of bartending. It's the bartender's *responsibility* to see that every customer's visit be as relaxing and as enjoyable as possible. Anyone with a little practice, can become polished in the field of customer relations by consistently practicing the following rules:

1) *Receive each customer with a smile and a warm greeting.*

A smile always makes a customer feel welcome and, as a result of feeling welcome, *relaxed.*

2) *Greet each new customer by "Sir" or "Madam."*

Remember the customer is paying for the privilege of being *served.*

3) *Learn each customer's name as soon as possible.*

Never forget that each person (including yourself) considers his or her name to be the sweetest sound in the world.

4) *Your job is to listen.*

You must realize that people are *always* much, much, much more interested in talking about themselves and their own opinions than they are in listening to you. People go to bars to have someone listen to their thoughts not to listen to someone else's.

Encourage your customers to talk—ask questions, and above all, be a good listener.

5) *Never enter into conversations uninvited.*

If two customers are enjoying a conversation, leave them alone. If they aren't talking, encourage them to, *then leave them alone.*

6) *Avoid arguments.*

If you have a conflicting opinion, *keep it to yourself.* If two customers start arguing, enter the conversation quickly and change the subject.

7) *Never let customers feel ignored.*

Let all feel they're getting equal attention. If a customer wants to be left alone, fine, but keep a close eye on his or her ashtray and glass; you should still give excellent service.

8) *Never talk about other customers.*

Avoid getting yourself into a position of being misquoted.

9) *If you have to leave the bar, excuse yourself.*

Customers don't like to be left alone; they feel ignored and uncomfortable.

10) *Always be in a good mood.*

People always prefer being with a friendly, enjoyable person. If a customer should ask how you are, always respond, "Fine, thank you."

11) *Always thank the customer sincerely.*

The customer should feel that you *truthfully* appreciated his or her patronage.

Bar Etiquette

Professional bartenders pride themselves on the continual use of proper etiquette. On duty, bartenders should make a conscious effort to always conduct themselves in a proper, astute manner. All the rules of etiquette listed below should be reviewed and memorized.

Personal Appearance
1) Always be well groomed.
2) Always keep your uniform clean and ironed and always keep your shoes polished.
3) Avoid combing or brushing your hair while behind the bar.
4) Always keep your hands and fingernails very clean.

Posture and Manner
1) Always stand erect and maintain good posture.
2) Never eat, chew gum, or smoke while on duty.
3) *Never* drink alcoholic beverages while on duty.
4) Never drink out of a liquor glass.
5) Never read books, magazines, or newspapers behind the bar.
6) If you cough or sneeze, turn your back, and then immediately wash your hands.

Preparing and Serving Cocktails
1) Never handle ice with your hands, always use a scoop.
2) Serve each drink with a fresh napkin, glass, and garnish.
3) Always keep your fingers away from the lips of the glasses.
4) If the customer desires coffee, always offer cream and sugar and always keep the cup filled.

5) Serve *each* bottle of beer with a fresh glass and pour the first glass for the customer.

6) Each time you serve a drink, *thank the customer.*

Cleaning

1) Always keep the bar top polished and the ashtrays cleaned.

2) Promptly replace soiled napkins.

3) Clean and replace spilled drinks immediately to minimize customer embarrassment.

Customer Relations

1) Never use poor language and never allow anyone to insult or embarrass other customers with loud, vulgar language.

2) Never guess at recipes. If you're not sure of a recipe inform the customer.

3) If a customer complains about a drink, apologize and immediately prepare a new cocktail.

THE OTHER HALF OF BARTENDING

Besides using proper etiquette, maintaining a good rapport with customers, and preparing mixed drinks, there is another *half* of bartending that too many bartenders fail to realize exists. Bartenders are also responsible for keeping the entire bar *clean, stocked,* and *well organized.*

Cleaning

Keeping the bar clean requires a continual effort by all bartenders. Properly managed bars establish a general routine similar to the one outlined below.

Every Day the Following Areas Should be Cleaned:

1) The bottles in the display case

2) The bar stools

3) The bar top
4) The cash register
5) The beer drain
6) The service station
7) The sinks
8) All of the stainless steel
9) The floors and drain sinks
10) The floor slats
11) The ice bins

At Least Once a Week the Following Areas Should be Cleaned:

1) All of the mirrors
2) All of the cabinetry
3) The entire top of the back bar
4) The steps and mirrors in the display case
5) The walls and shelves of the refrigerator
6) All of the trash cans
7) The ice storage bin
8) The beer cooler
9) The coffee warmer

Organization

As the old saying goes, "A place for everything and everything in its place." Nothing frustrates a busy bartender more than to *hunt* for supplies. All bartenders should follow these rules:

1) Always keep the display case properly organized.
2) Keep each style of glassware in its appropriate area.
3) In the refrigerators, keep the garnishes, fruit juices, pre-mixes, and dairy products properly organized.
4) Wash and dry the dirty glasses immediately.
5) Keep all of the equipment (mixing glasses, mixing cans, strainers, mixing spoons, etc.) in its appropriate place.
6) Keep all of the mixes (bitters, bouillon, sugar, etc.) well organized.

7) Keep the bar checks arranged in a orderly manner.

8) Keep the bar drawer clean.

9) Keep the glass towels and bar towels folded or hung in their proper places.

Stocking

There is no need for a bartender ever to run out of any supplies, because the bar should always be well stocked. All bartenders should spend at least the last hour of their shifts stocking the bar for the next bartender. There should always be backup supplies of:

1) All garnishes

2) All fruit juices

3) All pre-mixes

4) All food items (creams, sugar, Tabasco, etc.)

5) All bar supplies (napkins, straws, stirs, etc.)

6) Bar and glass towels

These rules will give you a general idea of the areas that need continual attention. You'll do well if you memorize and always abide by these three rules:

1) After using *anything* always return it to its proper place.

2) Always be prepared by *continually* checking and restocking backup supplies.

3) Never spend your free time standing idle, spend it cleaning and polishing the bar.

BAR ORGANIZATION

Obviously, all bars are built differently, but as a rule they are usually arranged in a manner somewhat similar to the diagrams presented here.

Figure 37 illustrates the different general areas of the bar. Following is a description of the design and use of each area.

Figure 38 gives a detailed illustration of the *well area*. This is the bartender's primary work area. While studying this diagram, keep in mind that the bottle arrangement is typical but by no means standard or mandatory.

GENERAL BAR ORGANIZATION

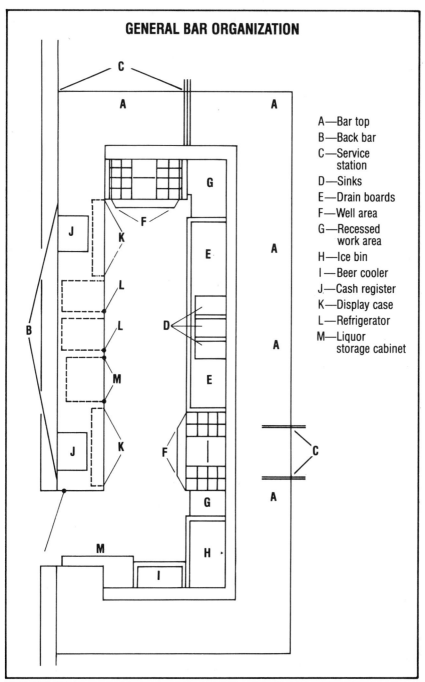

A—Bar top
B—Back bar
C—Service
   station
D—Sinks
E—Drain boards
F—Well area
G—Recessed
   work area
H—Ice bin
I—Beer cooler
J—Cash register
K—Display case
L—Refrigerator
M—Liquor
   storage cabinet

FIGURE 37

TOP VIEW OF WELL AREA

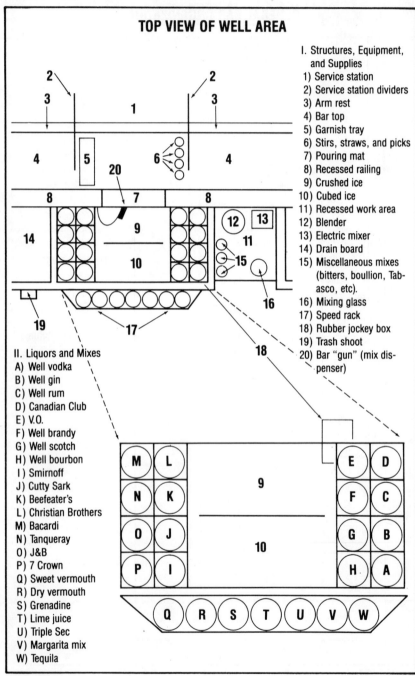

I. Structures, Equipment, and Supplies
1) Service station
2) Service station dividers
3) Arm rest
4) Bar top
5) Garnish tray
6) Stirs, straws, and picks
7) Pouring mat
8) Recessed railing
9) Crushed ice
10) Cubed ice
11) Recessed work area
12) Blender
13) Electric mixer
14) Drain board
15) Miscellaneous mixes (bitters, boullion, Tabasco, etc).
16) Mixing glass
17) Speed rack
18) Rubber jockey box
19) Trash shoot
20) Bar "gun" (mix dispenser)

II. Liquors and Mixes
A) Well vodka
B) Well gin
C) Well rum
D) Canadian Club
E) V.O.
F) Well brandy
G) Well scotch
H) Well bourbon
I) Smirnoff
J) Cutty Sark
K) Beefeater's
L) Christian Brothers
M) Bacardi
N) Tanqueray
O) J&B
P) 7 Crown
Q) Sweet vermouth
R) Dry vermouth
S) Grenadine
T) Lime juice
U) Triple Sec
V) Margarita mix
W) Tequila

FIGURE 38

The exact bottle arrangement will vary with each bar, and the majority of bars will allow the bartender to arrange the bottles in the *well area* in any manner that he or she feels is most convenient. (Remember, this shifting of bottles pertains only to the well area; the organization of the display case should always remain constant.)

Generally speaking, all bars keep all of the *well liquor* and the most commonly requested *call liquor* stored in the *well area*.

General Bar Organization

A) *BAR TOP*—The **bar top** is generally made up of three areas. First, there is the padded railing on the customers side that's called the **arm rest**. Then there is the main part of the **bar top**, upon which the customer is served cocktails. Finally, there is a slightly recessed shelf on the bartender's side, which is used to store clean ashtrays, folded bar towels, and dirty glasses (temporarily).

B) *BACK BAR*—The **back bar** (the area directly behind the bartender) is used to store clean glassware, liquor displays, and cash registers.

C) *SERVICE STATION*—This area is used by waiters and waitresses to order cocktails from the bartender. It's usually bordered on both sides to separate it from the rest of the bar. Napkins, cocktail trays, and all garnishes are stored in the **service station**.

D) *SINKS*—There are three **sinks** commonly used to clean glassware. The first sink contains brushes and hot detergent water. The second sink contains hot rinse water, and the last sink contains hot water treated with disinfectant. Because the water in all of these sinks tends to rapidly cool down and become dirty, bartenders should be constantly draining and refilling the sinks.

E) *DRAIN BOARDS*—After the glasses are cleaned, they are placed upside down on a drain board. On the drain board, the rinse water drips off and the glasses practically dry before being polished by the bartender.

F) *WELL AREA*—The bartender's primary work area. Illustrated in detail in Figure 38.

G) *RECESSED WORK AREA*—This area is normally used to store all equipment and miscellaneous mixes.

H) *ICE BIN*—This is where all the backup ice is stored (cubed and crushed).

I) *BEER COOLER*—The storage area for all bottled beer.

J) *CASH REGISTERS*—There is usually one register for each **service station**.

K) *DISPLAY CASE*—There area in which the remainder of the open liquor inventory is stored.

L) *REFRIGERATOR*—The storage area for all chilled glassware, chilled liquors and wines, garnishes, premixes, and food items (cream, fruit juices, etc.).

M) *LIQUOR STORAGE CABINET*—Storage area for all backup supplies of liquor.

Mix Gun

Mix guns are commonly used in most bars. The mixes are stored in tanks and dispensed through a hand held "gun" with the use of carbon dioxide gas.

The use of the hand dispenser greatly aids the efficiency of a bartender by allowing him or her to dispense any mix by simply pushing the appropriate button. This eliminates the awkwardness of storing and using a large number of bottled mixes.

Mix guns come in a wide variety of sizes (usually with five to seven buttons) and can dispense any mix. The dispenser diagramed in Figure 39 is typical, although the sweetsour mix is still normally poured out of a bottle.

Liquor Gun

Liquor dispensers are becoming more popular because of the added controls they offer. These guns can be adjusted to dispense any quantity of liquor desired, and most are equipped with counters which keep records on the number of portions dispensed.

A bartender using both guns can increase efficiency by holding the **mix gun** in the left hand, and the **liquor gun** in the right, using both at the same time.

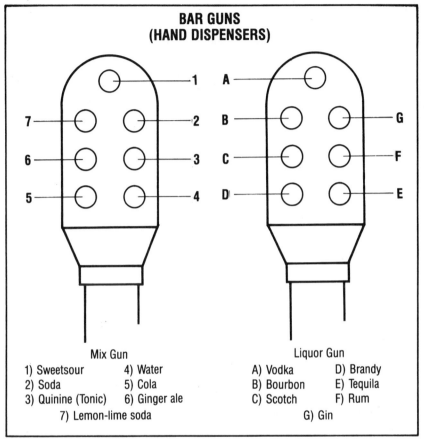

FIGURE 39

You'll find that the arrangement of the buttons will vary with each dispenser. The arrangement in these diagrams are typical but not necessarily standard.

THE FINAL TWO STEPS
TO PROFESSIONAL BARTENDING

After you've mastered the preceding material on bartending, and have practiced and researched, you'll know everything a professional bartender should.

Practice

Continual practice can not be emphasized enough. In an effort to fully retain all of the knowledge you've learned, you'll need to read the sections of this chapter at least three more times.

You'll also need to spend a great deal of time concentrating on each of the following four areas.

1) *PRIMARY COCKTAILS*

Continually practice with your flash cards until these cocktails become second nature.

2) *SECONDARY COCKTAILS*

3) *THE JIGGER*

You'll need to spend at least a half hour each day practicing the various techniques listed.

4) *TESTS*

To strengthen your memory, continually review the training tests listed in the appendix.

Research

It's amazing how much you can learn by simply going to a well organized bar and watching a professional bartender work. When going to a bar, I suggest you sit at the stool next to the waiter/waitress service station.

Pay close attention to the following:

1) *ANALYZE THE LIQUOR INVENTORY*

Try to read each label and if you notice an unfamiliar name ask the bartender what it is.

Notice how the various types of liquors are grouped together and try to determine if the bar is well organized.

2) *ANALYZE THE GENERAL ARRANGEMENT OF THE BAR*

Try to identify each of the areas listed and illustrated.

3) *INSPECT THE GLASSWARE*

See if you can identify each of the fifteen types of glassware listed.

4) *DETERMINE THE SKILL OF THE BARTENDER*

Analyze the bartender in all areas of barmanship. Is he or she well organized? Is the bar top kept clean? Are the cocktails properly prepared? Does he or she always use proper etiquette?

By analyzing all of the actions of the bartender, you can learn to distinguish between the many good and bad habits that he or she has learned to use.

5) *LISTEN TO THE WAITERS AND WAITRESSES ORDERING COCKTAILS*

See if you can understand the orders and see if the servers garnish their cocktails properly.

6) *IF YOU FEEL THE BARTENDER IS A TRUE PROFESSIONAL, TALK WITH HIM OR HER ABOUT BARTENDING*

You'll find that most bartenders enjoy discussing their own theories about bartending. Be careful about any advice they may offer; most bartenders are not nearly the authorities they would like you to believe!

It's important that you obtain a well rounded education by researching the operations of a number of bars and bartenders. Try to only go to those bars that have a good reputation (fine restaurants, large hotels, etc.).

Chapter 6

TRAINING PROGRAMS IN GENERAL

The success of a bar operation is almost entirely dependent on the quality of its employees. Therefore, establishing sound employee training programs is immensely important and might even be considered the foundation of successful bar management.

Besides giving the manager the freedom to employ inexperienced help, thorough training programs also eliminate the months of aggravation and confusion that always arise from misunderstandings or misinterpretations of rules. One of the most overlooked, yet important reasons for a quality training program is that it gives the new employee an excellent first impression of the organization of the bar or restaurant. It has been well confirmed that first impressions are critically important in determining an employee's eventual success or failure as a worker.

A complete training program can be surveyed in three sections, *hiring policies*, *job training*, and *motivational techniques*.

HIRING POLICIES

The first step in establishing a program is to obtain quality trainees through sound hiring policies. Teaching any subject is substantially easier when the students are open-minded and possess a positive attitude.

The Primary Objective

It's highly desirable to establish hiring objectives which are primarily based on the general attitude of the applicants rather than the quality of their experience. In other words, it's normally far better to choose employees on the basis of how readily they'll respond to training rather than how well they've been trained by someone else.

Unfortunately, this method of hiring can be effective only if the employer has a sound training program in operation—a program complete enough to be capable of producing fully competent employees in a short period of time.

Without doubt, the most common mistake in hiring is the practice of selecting applicants entirely on the basis of their experience. The primary objective should always be to acquire employees with the proper attitude, specifically employees who are *open-minded* and *motivated.*

New employees should be open and willing to accept that all rules are absolutely firm and must be adhered to without exception. They must accept that some rules will be different than they are used to and that, in an effort to conform, they may have to change their work habits. Those with previous experience sometimes find this transition difficult, but this is an area in which management must remain firm. New employees must be open-minded about adjusting to new rules and policies, and must realize that all of the rules have been established for a reason and that none will be adjusted for any employee, new or old.

New employees should also be motivated. They should be sincerely interested in the exact position available and should be enthusiastic about the training program, their rate of pay, their job responsibilities, and the establishment itself. Management should always be hesitant to hire applicants who are less than fully satisfied with any aspect of the specific job they are applying for. Discontent has a tendency to grow and produces employees who are difficult to train and hard to motivate.

The Secondary Objective

The secondary objective in hiring is to obtain employees with both sound employment histories and, if possible, comparable experience.

The soundness of an applicant's employment history is of critical importance. Even if previous employment was in unrelated fields, the factors of *stability, quality of employment,* and *reason for termination* should be closely analyzed.

The true value of comparable experience is directly related to both the specific job and the quality of the established training program. For example, if you had a position open that would require either hiring an experienced applicant or spending several months training an inexperienced applicant, the value of experience would obviously be immense. If, on the other hand, through the use of an effective training program, an inexperienced employee could be trained to handle the same position within two weeks, the value of the previous experience would be greatly diminished. A high quality training program has the effect of significantly reducing the value of experience.

Experience is a desirable attribute, but it can be overemphasized and it is always of secondary importance when compared to attitude.

Successful Interviewing

One of the keys to successful hiring is to develop successful interviewing techniques. It's much easier to make a realistic evaluation of an applicant through the use of a structured, well organized interviewing format.

A manager should never enter an interview intending only to scrutinize the applicant's employment record in detail. The value of a personal interview lies in the fact that it gives the manager the opportunity to appraise the applicant's character. Therefore, the actual line of questioning should at first deal only with the primary objective, evaluating the applicant's attitude.

Only after it has been determined that the applicant is open-minded and is sincerely enthusiastic about the specific job available, the rate of pay, the training program, and the job responsibilities, should the line of questioning be shifted toward evaluating the applicant's work history.

An interview sheet is a printed form which is used to help the manager with the organization of the interview. It contains a list of general questions on topics which must be discussed in detail before an applicant can be hired. By covering each question on the interview sheet, a manager can be assured of a thorough interview. The actual printed questions can be reworded and should be expanded upon in an effort to keep the interview on a relaxed, personal level. The sheet also offers blank spaces which should be used for notes. An interview sheet used in interviewing bartenders is shown in Figure 40. The interview sheet would of course be reworked for different jobs and circumstances.

After the interview, the interview sheet should be stapled with the completed application and filed.

JOB TRAINING

The next phase of a complete training program would be job training. This is the preliminary portion of training which introduces the new employees to the detailed rules and responsibilities associated with their new job. Depending on the job and the quality of the employee, this portion of training can last from a few days to a few weeks.

To insure that the *quality* of training remains consistent, it's imperative that the *trainers* and the *exact methods* of training remain consistent. This can only be done through selecting and teaching key employees to aid in training, and by establishing, in writing, a set training format.

The Trainers

There should only be two trainers: one should be the manager and the other a designated employee. If at all possible, the manager should do the major part of the training. It's very important to establish a good line of communication between the manager and the new employee during the first few days of employment. This policy will usually result in the new employee having a much clearer understanding of his or her responsibilities.

The other trainer should be a designated employee who has been properly trained in the exact techniques to be used in teaching new employees. It's important that the employee/trainers are well prepared and realize the importance of being consistent with management on the points of emphasis during training. The employee trainer should only be used during the on-the-job training phase of the program.

There should be an employee trainer within each area of liquor service: a bartender, a cocktail server, and a food server. In selecting these trainers a priority should be placed on their natural ability to communicate, their knowledge of the job, and their compatibility with management.

BARTENDER'S
INTERVIEW SHEET

NAME: _____

DATE: _____

CHARACTER

1) We emphasize consistency in our bar operation and therefore we require our new bartenders to memorize our bar manual before starting work. As a result, you may have to learn to prepare and garnish cocktails in a manner you're not used to. Are you open-minded about changing your work habits?

2) How do you feel about having to memorize a bar manual?

3) We require all of our bartenders, regardless of their experience, to participate in a five day training period which ends with a written test. Do you mind devoting a week to training?

4) How do you feel about taking a written test?

5) To insure consistency, management keeps a close eye on the bar. Are you apprehensive about working under close supervision? Does constructive criticism bother you?

6) The exact schedule open is _____ and your starting rate of pay would be _____. Does that sound like a position that you'd be interested in? Are there any conflicts in the schedule?

COMMENTS:

WORK HISTORY

1) What type of supervision are you used to?

2) What did your previous manager emphasize most? (Speed, quality, cleanliness, customer relations, etc.)

3) Did you feel you were well managed?   Why?

4) What type of clientele are you used to?

5) Have you ever had problems with customers?

6) What type of sales volume are you used to?

7) What was the reason you left your last job? And the previous job?

COMMENTS:

MANAGER: _____

FIGURE 40

The Training Format

A training format should consist of the proper balance of oral explanation, written study material, actual on-the-job training, and testing.

Teaching the Rules

The first phase of training should be handled exclusively by the manager and should be dedicated to a thorough explanation of all the rules and responsibilities pertaining to the new employee's job. Besides simply explaining what the rules are, the manager should also take the time to fully explain the logic behind each rule. This added explanation will add to the retention of what the employee is being taught.

In an effort to immediately rectify any misunderstanding, particular emphasis should be placed on details and the new employee should be continually encouraged to ask questions. This orientation period is critically important and the manager must be assured that the trainee fully understands each rule and job responsibility before being allowed to proceed to the on-the-job training phase of the program.

Printed Study Material

Printed study material is an invaluable aid in an employee training program. It aids the trainees by giving them the opportunity to complement their training with home study and by relieving them of the necessity of taking notes. If the material is complete, it'll aid the manager by acting as a guarantee that all of the rules have been well presented. Finally, and possibly most importantly, having all of the rules in print has the psychological effect on the employee of increasing the rules' importance.

The study material should be issued after the rule explanation period and should be continually referred to throughout the program.

On-the-Job Training

This portion of training is handled by the designated employee/trainer. The trainee simply follows the employee/trainer through a typical work day. This offers the trainee the opportunity to witness exactly how the rules are implemented and to ask questions on the spot. Again the trainee should be continually encouraged to ask questions.

This phase of training can be exceptionally valuable, but only if the employee/trainer is well prepared by the manager and emphasizes details.

Testing

The final phase of training should be a written test. Besides offering the manager actual proof of the employee's knowledge, a written test is, more importantly, an excellent training aid. In fact, such a test should actually be thought of as a training tool rather than any form of final examination.

After the trainees have taken the test, regardless of the results, the manager should discuss with each of them the questions which were answered incorrectly. This will give the manager a final opportunity to clarify any misunderstandings before the trainee actually starts working.

There should be an established score which the trainee must achieve before being allowed to work. If the trainee fails the test, yet still shows potential, the manager should review with the trainee the incorrectly answered questions and allow the test to be taken at a later date. Once the test has been passed and the incorrect answers again reviewed, the trainee should be fully prepared to start working.

The final test should be signed by the trainee and kept on file by the manager. In the event of any future rule violations, the manager can be assured that the employee was originally aware of the rules.

MOTIVATIONAL TECHNIQUES

During the initial training period, new employees will normally maintain a high degree of motivation. They'll be participating in a learning process and preparing themselves for a test. Unfortunately, if after this original training period employees are not given further training and higher goals, they'll eventually find their jobs to be routine, lose interest, and the quality of their work will begin to deteriorate.

To prevent this, employees must realize that passing the written test does not symbolize the end of their training. Such areas as customer relations, proper etiquette and manner, and general organization are areas they'll have to continually improve on.

To insure that all employees continually make an effort to increase the quality of their work, the manager should employ a number of motivational techniques. Group meetings, salary incentive programs, periodic personal job evaluations, and employee contests can all be examples of such techniques.

This particular phase of training is critical, yet often overlooked. Regardless of how well employees are originally trained, their eventual performance will only be equal to their level of motivation.

Chapter 7

BARTENDERS

HIRING POLICIES IN GENERAL

When interviewing perspective bartenders, a manager must always keep in mind that a bartender assumes far more responsibilities than the average employee. Besides performing their basic duties of preparing and serving cocktails, maintaining good customer relations, and keeping the bar clean and well organized, bartenders are also responsible for:

1) Always abiding by the state laws associated with operating with a liquor license.
2) Properly handling customer problems that arise at the bar or in the lounge.
3) Maintaining an established liquor cost.
4) Controlling the liquor inventory.
5) Taking cash and operating a cash register.
6) Seeing that all employees follow the house rules pertaining to the bar and cocktail lounge.
7) Overseeing food servers and cocktail servers ordering and garnishing their cocktails properly.

Because it's often difficult for managers to spend much time in the cocktail lounge, they must delegate to the bartenders the responsibility of seeing that state laws and house policies are always adhered to.

As stated earlier, it's very important that all new employees are open-minded and enthusiastic about their new jobs, but when dealing with bartenders their ability to assume responsibility is an equally important factor.

Hiring Inexperienced Bartenders

The biggest disadvantage in hiring an inexperienced bartender lies in the cost and time involved in training. A trainee bartender will need at least two weeks of solid training and even then will usually only be qualified enough to work the slowest shifts. Therefore, many managers argue that the initial training cost is too great and because the preliminary training program produces less than a fully qualified bartender, hiring inexperienced bartenders is simply not practical.

On the other hand, there are advantages in hiring trainee bartenders. First, the manager can hire strictly on the basis of stability and reliability, without having to be heavily concerned with the applicant's practical experience. Managers who prefer this policy will also argue that inexperienced bartenders tend to be more open-minded about learning new rules and recipes, as they have nothing to "unlearn." They reason that the original training cost can be fully recovered within eight weeks by paying the trainee bartender at a reduced hourly rate, and if the new bartender is given further training through that eight-week period, he or she should be almost fully competent while still being paid at a reduced rate. Considering this, it can be argued that hiring inexperienced bartenders is actually profitable, not costly!

The advantages and disadvantages must be weighed by the individual manager, but with regards to hiring trainee bartenders the following three rules should always be adhered to.

1) Never hire a trainee bartender without first establishing a full training program. This includes having a fully detailed bar manual and a competent employee trainer.
2) Hire only trainees who are interested in studying and working hard in an effort to make their training period as short as possible.
3) Trainees must possess the same basic requirements as experienced bartenders in that they must be open-minded, enthusiastic and responsible.

Hiring Experienced Bartenders

The manager who has neither the time nor the training program will be forced to hire only experienced bartenders. The key to success in this situation is to properly evaluate an applicant's experience. The three most important factors to consider are, in order, quality, stability, and time.

Quality

Quality refers to both the previous employer and the responsibilities associated with the previous job. Bartenders from respected, well managed establishments will probably have been well trained and will normally bring with them good work habits. Unfortunately, the most expensive restaurants, hotels, and nightclubs are not always the best managed; therefore a manager will have to question all applicants about their previous management and the responsibilities with their previous jobs.

Stability

A history of stability is a highly desirable attribute in any new employee, but especially in bartenders. As a rule, long term employees seem to have a greater sense of responsibility than those who are continually changing jobs, and responsibility is possibly the most desirable attribute in a new bartender.

Time

The length of a bartender's experience is important, but is usually far overweighed. A bartender's ten years of experience is in no way a guarantee that he or she will be any more qualified than a bartender with two years of experience. Again the key is the quality of the experience. A bartender with long-term experience working under quality management will often display a greater degree of professionalism and will usually be more adept at handling customer problems than will a less experienced bartender. On the other hand, bartenders with long term experience working under poor management may conduct themselves in an unprofessional manner and be more difficult to train than a less experienced bartender.

The Interview Sheet

There are areas that must be openly discussed during the interview before a manager can make a realistic evaluation of a perspective bartender.

Not only is it imperative that the manager gain as much information as possible before making a final decision, it's equally important that the applicant have a clear picture of the responsibilities she or he'll be undertaking before accepting the job.

As a result, it's critical that the manager give each applicant a complete well structured interview. This task is not as easy as it may seem, so to guarantee consistency it's an excellent idea for the manager to use an interview sheet similar to the one in Figure 40, on page 181.

The questions are all very general and should each be expanded upon. The manager should also feel free to rephrase the questions in an effort to keep the interview on a personal level.

JOB TRAINING
Training Experienced Bartenders

In constructing a training schedule, the primary concerns should be time and expense. It should be possible to fully train an experienced bartender within five working days and at an expense of a week's wages for a new bartender. The training schedule outlined below is based on 30 hours.

Day One: Job Orientation

The first day of training need only last two to three hours and should be conducted exclusively by the manager. It should deal with teaching the new bartender all of the rules and responsibilities associated with the job. Because of the number and the importance of the responsibilities that a new bartender will be assuming, this is an area of training that the manager cannot afford to delegate.

Below is an outline of the topics that should be discussed.

General Employee Rules and Policies

1) Employees and the bar

2) Employee meals

3) The time clock

4) Breaks

5) Changing shifts

6) Absenteeism

7) Dress code

8) Vacations

9) Employee benefits

10) Levels of management

Specific Job Rules and Responsibilities

1) Portion controls and liquor cost

2) Memorizing the bar manual

3) State laws

4) Customer relations

5) Working with food servers

6) Working with cocktail servers

7) The cash register

8) Proper etiquette

9) Bar checks and food checks

10) Cleaning responsibilities

The Training Schedule

1) Day by day outline of responsibilities

2) Theory behind testing

3) Introduction to the training bartender

If the manager discusses each of these topics in detail she or he'll be assured that the new bartender will be fully aware of the responsibilities of the job.

Day Two: Following

The second day of training consists of the trainee following and observing the training bartender (day bartender) through a typical work day. The trainee

should be encouraged to ask questions regarding any aspect of the job.
The following topics should be discussed in detail:

1) The organization of the bar
2) The locations of all backup supplies (liquor, beer, wine, bar supplies, food supplies, cleaning supplies, and ice.)
3) The steps in opening and closing the bar.
4) Cleaning responsibilities
5) Glassware

After the second day of training the new bartender should have a clear understanding of the organization and general operating procedures of the bar.

Days Three and Four: Working Under Supervision

Throughout the third and fourth days of training the trainee should assume the role and all of the responsibilities of the day bartender, while working under the supervision of the training bartender. During these two days, the training bartender should strictly enforce all rules and continually emphasize consistency.

After each day the trainer should report to the manager on the progress of the new bartender.

Day Five: Evaluation and Testing

If the trainer determines that the new bartender is fully competent, the manager will evaluate the new bartender's knowledge through a written test.

If the trainer determines that the new bartender needs further training, the test will be postponed and the manager will decide if the training should be extended and, if so, for how long.

Once the written test has been satisfactorily completed and the mistakes have been reviewed, the training will conclude and the new bartender will be placed on a short probation period.

The actual testing and evaluation period on day five should last only about two hours. If the new bartender passes the test, he or she should be qualified enough to work the remainder of the day unsupervised.

Training Inexperienced Bartenders

It will usually take between two and three weeks of time to fully train an inexperienced bartender. The ability of the trainer and the enthusiasm of the trainee will play important roles in determining the success of such a program.

The training schedule briefly outlined below is based on 12 working days or eighty-six hours.

Job Orientation

The first day of training should last about three hours and should be very similar to the first day of training an experienced bartender. It should be conducted exclusively by the manager and deal with a thorough explanation of all of the rules and responsibilities that the new bartender will be assuming.

The actual topics of discussion should be identical to those outlined in the experienced bartenders training schedule.

Week One: Following and Home Study

For an entire week the trainee should follow and observe the training bartender throughout typical work days. At night the trainee should add to the training by studying and memorizing the bar manual.

Throughout the week, the trainer should conduct detailed discussions on the following topics:

1) General organization of the bar
2) The tools of bartending
3) Opening and closing the bar
4) Categories of liquors
5) Proper etiquette
6) Cleaning responsibilities
7) Customer relations
8) Portion controls and liquor cost
9) Cash register operation
10) Check controls

11) Theory behind pricing
12) State laws
13) Working with food servers
14) Working with cocktail servers
15) Increasing speed and efficiency

Throughout the first week, the trainee should be encouraged to ask questions, take notes and study hard at night.

Week Two: Supervised Work

Throughout the second week, the trainee should assume the role and all of the responsibilities of the day bartender, while working under his or her close supervision.

During the slow periods of each day, the trainer should test the trainee's memory through oral tests on recipes, prices, brands of liquor, house rules and state laws. This continual testing will greatly add to the trainee's awareness.

A great deal of emphasis should be placed on details and the bar manual should be continually referred to.

Final Day: Evaluation and Testing

The final day of training should be conducted in exactly the same manner as the final day of an experienced bartender's training. If the trainer determines that the trainee has made satisfactory progress, the manager should issue the written test and evaluate the trainee's knowledge. If the test is passed and the mistakes reviewed, the trainee should be ready to assume a bartender's schedule.

Printed Training Material

A detailed bar manual is a very desirable asset to any bar because it performs two very important tasks. First, it eliminates misunderstandings by listing all house rules and recipes, and, secondly, it supplies new bartenders with all the printed material they'll need.

A complete bar manual should contain each of the following nine sections:

Portion Controls. A description of how all liquor should be measured and the exact portions in which all liquor should be served.

Standard Recipes. A list of recipes for the most commonly ordered cocktails. Each recipe should include the type of glassware, the type of ice, the method of preparation, the exact measurements of all ingredients, and the garnish.

House Drinks and Premixes. A special list of recipes for house drinks and house premixes.

Garnishes. A description of how each garnish should be cut, stored and served.

Shift Responsibilities. In order to keep the bar clean and well organized, each shift will have to perform specific duties. This section should outline those duties.

General House Policies. A list of general house policies pertaining to the bar and cocktail lounge.

General Etiquette. A list of basic rules of etiquette that all bartenders will be responsible for following.

Price List. A fully detailed list of prices for all liquor, wine, beer, mixed drinks, and soft drinks.

Ordering Abbreviations. A list of ordering abbreviations that will be used by food and cocktail servers.

The recipe section and instructions on garnishes may be similar to the one presented in Chapter 5, or the bar owner may simply keep on hand the cocktail recipe book he or she prefers. One approach to the rest of the material was developed in the following bar manual sections.

Shift Responsibilities

Each shift will be responsible for completing certain duties pertaining to the cleanliness and organization of the bar. The daily completion of these responsibilities will guarantee that the bar will always be maintained in the proper manner.

The Day Shift

Opening
1) Check the busboy's cleaning duties. (The bar floor should be

mopped, the wooden slates cleaned, the trash emptied, the trash cans cleaned, the lounge vacuumed, and the ice bins should be filled.)

2) Check the liquor inventory. If there is any item not at par the manager should be notified.

Stocking

1) Check the supply of juices (orange, grapefruit, etc.) and dairy products (cream, milk, whipped cream, etc.). The freshness of these items must be checked daily. It's the day bartender's responsibility to see that these items are correctly rotated and that any spoiled items are immediately discarded.

2) Check the supply of cut fruits (limes, oranges, lemons, celery, etc.). Only fresh fruit will be used; any wilted fruit should be discarded. The day bartender will be responsible for the proper rotation of cut fruits.

3) Check the supply of all bar supplies (grenadine, lime juice, Mai Tai mix, etc.). If any of these items are in short supply notify the manager.

4) Get clean ashtrays from the dishwasher and clean towels from the manager.

Cleaning

1) The bar top should be polished and the arm rests cleaned.

2) The bar stools should be organized and wiped down.

3) The back bar should be clean and appear well organized.

4) The garnish tray and all of the back up containers should be cleaned.

Besides these minor cleaning duties, the day bartender will also be responsible for following a general cleaning schedule. Each day the day shift will be responsible for thoroughly cleaning a specific area of the bar, as outlined below:

General Cleaning Schedule

MONDAY—THOROUGHLY CLEAN ONE REFRIGERATOR

One refrigerator should be completely emptied and cleaned. This includes the refrigerator door, walls, and shelving.

TUESDAY—CLEAN ALL OF THE MIRRORS AND POLISH THE BOTTLES

All of the mirrors should be cleaned with window spray and all of the bottles in the display case should be polished with a clean dry towel.

WEDNESDAY—POLISH ALL OF THE CABINETS AND SHELVING

All of the cabinets and shelving on the back bar should be wiped down and polished with furniture polish.

THURSDAY—CLEAN THE BACK BAR AND POLISH THE BOTTLES

The glassware should be moved and the entire back bar and cash register should be polished. The bottles in the display case should also be polished.

FRIDAY—CLEAN THE DISPLAY CASE

All of the bottles should be removed and the display case should be thoroughly cleaned.

SATURDAY—POLISH THE STAINLESS STEEL

All of the stainless steel should be cleaned and polished—specifically corners and areas that are normally missed.

SUNDAY—POLISH THE BOTTLES AND CHECK THE FLOOR

On Sundays the busboy will do a thorough job of sweeping and mopping the bar. The bartender should check this and check the entire organization of the bar floor. It should be immaculate. The bottles in the display case should also be polished.

The Night Shift

Cleaning

Each night after the bar closes the night bartender will be responsible for the following cleaning duties:

1) Melt the ice down and clean the ice bins.
2) Drain and clean the sinks.
3) Wipe all of the stainless steel down.
4) Send the ashtrays to the dishwasher.
5) Gather the dirty towels and put them in the dirty linen bag back in the kitchen.

6) Clean and dry all of the equipment (blender, mixing can, etc.)

7) Clean and dry all glassware and store them in their appropriate place.

8) Wipe down the bar top.

9) Put the garnish tray away and wipe down the service station.

10) Clean the speed racks.

Besides these general duties, on Sunday nights the bartender should send the "jockey boxes"—the square rubber containers used to hold bottles upright—to the dishwasher to be cleaned. The busboy will return them in the morning.

Closing

1) All of the emptied bottles should be aligned on the bar top and the daily requisition sheet should be filled in.

2) All of the cabinets and drawers in the back bar should be locked.

In general, by the time the night bartender leaves the bar should be clean, organized, and ready for the following day.

General Rules and Policies Regarding the Bar and Cocktail Lounge

1) *DRINKING—Absolutely no employee will be allowed to consume an alcoholic beverage at any time* (on duty or off). This rule will be strictly enforced and any employee found drinking or even tasting an alcoholic beverage will be terminated. No employees are allowed to consume *any beverage* (alcoholic or nonalcoholic) out of a liquor glass.

2) *SMOKING*—Because many customers find smoking to be offensive, no employees are allowed to smoke while on duty. You may smoke during any of your breaks, but only in the employee eating area.

3) *EATING*—Eating is only allowed during breaks and only in the employee eating area. Eating is *never* allowed behind the bar.

4) *COMPLIMENTARY DRINKS*—No bartender is allowed to issue a complimentary drink *unless specifically authorized by the*

manager. All drinks must be immediately rung on the register after being served.

5) *INTOXICATED CUSTOMERS*—It's the bartender's responsibility to see that intoxicated customers are *never served additional liquor.* Any problems regarding such customers should be immediately brought to the manager's attention. Any bartender found intentionally serving obviously intoxicated customers will be terminated.

6) *CHECKING IDENTIFICATION*—There must never be any doubt of the customer being of age. All customers looking to be less than 25 years of age must have their age verified through proper identification. If there is any doubt as to the authenticity of the identification, it should immediately be brought to the manager's attention.

7) *EMPLOYEES IN THE LOUNGE*—No employees are allowed to needlessly linger around the bar or cocktail lounge. It's the bartender's responsibility to see that this rule is enforced.

8) *DRESS CODE*—Bartenders will always be expected to be well groomed and dressed to code. Clothes are expected to always be clean and ironed, and shoes should always be shined.

9) *WAITER/WAITRESS RELATIONS*—It's mandatory that bartenders always maintain a good rapport with waitresses and waiters. *Bickering and arguments will not be allowed.* Any misunderstandings should simply be brought to the manager's attention.

10) *FLOOR SERVICE—Food servers must be served as quickly as possible!* It's imperative to the operation of the restaurant that waiters and waitresses spend as little time as possible in the cocktail lounge and as much time as possible on the floor serving their customers.

11) *BAR STOOLS*—At no time should any employee sit or lean against a bar stool (on or off duty). The bartender on duty will be expected to heavily enforce this rule.

12) *CUSTOMER RELATIONS*—All customers should enjoy prompt, courteous service. If the bartender is busy, he or she should always acknowledge the presence of a new customer by saying, "Hello sir, I'll be with you in just one moment." All

customers should be greeted with a smile and the bartender should never forget the words *hello, goodbye,* and *thank you very much.* It's very important that when dealing with customers a bartender always conduct her or himself in a professional manner.

13) *CLEANLINESS OF THE BAR*—Each bartender must realize that keeping the bar clean and organized is one of the job's primary responsibilities. There is no excuse for the bar to ever be less than immaculate. A cleaning program has been designed to guarantee consistency in this area. Each shift will be responsible for completing specifically outlined cleaning duties.

14) *CONSISTENCY*—This manual was written to guarantee absolute consistency in both the quality of the drinks and the behavior and actions of the bartenders. *It's the bartenders responsibility to see that all of the rules, policies, and recipes outlined in this manual are strictly abided by.* Because there will always be a copy of the bar manual in the bar drawer, there will be no excuse for any deviations.

15) *BAR CHECKS*—Bar checks will be issued to the bartender daily, at the beginning of the shift. It's the bartender's responsibility to see that *all checks* are returned at the end of the shift. *All transactions taking place at the bar will be recorded on bar checks.*

16) *BAR SERVICE* (BRSV)—All drinks must be rung on the Bar Service key immediately after being served. *No drinks can leave the bar until they've been rung on the register, and a bartender should never start a new order before the previous order has been rung.*

17) *MISTAKES*—If a customer complains about a drink or if a food server returns a drink for any reason, a new drink will be made without hesitation. Continued complaints by any customer or continual mistakes by any waiter or waitress should be brought to the manager's attention. *There will be no attempt to save returned drinks for resale, they will be immediately thrown out.*

General Rules of Etiquette

It is mandatory that all bartenders follow these basic rules of etiquette.

1) Always stand erect and maintain good posture.
2) If you cough or sneeze, turn your back, and then immediately wash your hands.
3) Never handle ice with your hands, always use an ice scoop.
4) Serve each drink with a fresh napkin, glass, and garnish.
5) Serve each beer with a fresh cold glass.
6) When serving a cocktail or when removing an empty cocktail glass, always keep your fingers away from the lip of the glass.
7) Each time you serve a drink *thank the customer.*
8) If a customer complains about a drink, apologize and immediately prepare a new cocktail.
9) Clean and replace spilled drinks immediately to minimize customer embarrassment. Customers should never be charged for spilled drinks.
10) Promptly replace soiled napkins and dirty ashtrays.
11) Never brush or comb your hair while behind the bar.
12) Proper grooming includes clean hands and clean fingernails.
13) Never enter into customers' conversations uninvited.

Price List

Liquor

$1.40—*WELL LIQUOR* (Add 10 cents when served on the rocks)
  1.50—*CALL LIQUOR* (Add 10 cents when served on the rocks)

Jack Daniels	Beefeater's	J&B
V.O.	Tanqueray	Smirnoff
7 Crown	Bombay	Christian Bros.
Early Times	Gold Tequila	Bacardi
Canadian Club	Cutty Sark	Dark Rum
Jim Beam	Dewar's	Myers Rum
Murphys	Red Label	151 Rum

JUICE DRINKS

Screwdriver	Greyhound	Collins	Daiquiri
Bloody Mary	Whiskey Sour	Gimlet	Etc.

MARTINIS, MANHATTANS AND ROB ROYS

  1.75—*CORDIALS*

Crème de Cacao (Light and Dark)	Anisette
Crème de Menthe (Light and Green)	Triple Sec

Crème de Cassis   Sloe Gin
Curaçao (Orange and Blue)   Crème de Banana
Peppermint Schnapps   Crème de Noyaux
All Fruit Brandies (Peach, Apricot, Cherry, and Blackberry)
SHERRY AND DUBONNET
Harvey's Bristol Cream   Dry Sack
DRINKS WITH A LIQUOR AND A LIQUEUR
Margarita   Tequila Sunrise   Rusty Nail
Black Russian   Singapore Sling   Stinger   Etc.
BLENDED CREAM DRINKS
Grasshopper   Golden Dream
Pink Lady   Brandy Alexander
Pink Squirrel   Etc.
Golden Cadillac

1.85—*PREMIUM CALL LIQUOR* (Add 10 cents when served on the rocks)
Chivas Regal   Wild Turkey   Black Label   Crown Royal

2.00—*LIQUEURS AND COGNACS*
Grand Marnier   Tia Maria   Martell
Galliano   Amaretto   Hennessy
Kahlua   Benedictine
Drambuie   Courvosier
ALL COFFEE DRINKS
Irish Coffee   Calypso Coffee
Keoke Coffee   Mexican Coffee   Etc.

2.25—*TROPICAL DRINKS*
Mai Tai   Planter's Punch   Chi Chi
Zombie   Piña Colada   Scorpian   Etc.
ADD $0.50 FOR FRUIT (Strawberry Daiquiries, Peach Margaritas, Etc.)
DEDUCT $0.50 FOR ALL VIRGIN DRINKS (Virgin Marys, Virgin Daiquiries, Etc.)

Beer	Wine (House)	Other
$1.00—Michelob	**$3.50**—Liter	**$0.50**—Soft Drinks
0.80—Budweiser	**2.25**—½ Liter	**0.75**—Juice
Coors	**1.00**—Glass	**1.00**—Mineral Water
0.65—Draft (Millers)	**1.00**—Port	

Ordering Abbreviations

When ordering wine or cocktails, food and cocktail servers will always write their orders and use only those abbreviations listed below.

Well Liquor

V = Vodka	G = Gin	Sc = Scotch	Bdy = Brandy
B = Bourbon	R = Rum	Tq = Tequila	

Mixes

/S = Soda	/W = Water	/C = Cola
/T = Tonic	/7 = Seven Up	/g = Ginger Ale

Methods of Preparation

® = Rocks	Dry = Dry	Pl = Plain	Perf = Perfect
↑ = Up	Extra Dry = X Dry	Tall = Tall	☐ = On and Over

Cocktails, Beer and House Wine

Banana Daiquiri	Ban Daiq	Peach Daiquiri	Peach Daiq
Black Russian	Russian	Piña Colada	Colada
Bloody Mary	Mary	Presbyterian	Press
Brandy Alexander	Alexander	Rusty Nail	Nail
Gibson	Marti	Salty Dog	Dog
Grasshopper	Hopper	Screwdriver	Driver
Greyhound	Hound	Singapore Sling	Sling
Harvey Wallbanger	Banger	Strawberry Daiquiri	Straw Daiq

John Collins	J. Collins	Tom Collins	T. Collins
Manhattan	Man	Tequila Sunrise	Sunrise
Margarita	Maggie	Vodka Collins	V. Collins
Martini	Marti	Whiskey Sour	Sour
Old-Fashioned	Fashion		

Budweiser	Bud	Millers	Draft
Michelob	Mich	Millers Lite	Lite

Burgundy	Burg	Glass	g/
Chablis	Chab	Liter	LT/
Rosé	Rosé	Half Liter	½LT/

Shirley Temple	Temple	Seven Up	Pl 7
Cola	Pl C	Soda	Pl S

Call Liquor

Beefeater	Beef
Canadian Club	C.C.
Chivas Regal	Chivas
Cutty Sark	Cutty
Dewar's White Label	Dewar's
Early Times	Times
Jack Daniel's	Daniels
Jim Beam	Beam
Johnnie Walker Black Label	Black Label
Johnnie Walker Red Label	Red Label
José Cuervo	Cuervo
José Cuervo Gold	Gold
Seagram's Crown Royal	Crown Royal
Seagram's 7 Crown	7 Crown

Special Requests

If the customer should request a specific garnish, or that a cocktail be prepared in a special manner, it should be noted in parenthesis after the drink.

Second Orders

If a table should order a second round of cocktails, a horizontal line should be drawn under the first order and the second order should be printed under that line.

If the second order is identical to the first, the server will simply print the word *"reorder."*

Bottled Wines

Bottled wines should always be fully spelled out. The two sizes may be abbreviated as follows:

Full = Full bottle (fifth). *Half* = Half bottle (tenth).

TESTING

New bartenders are often quick to assure the manager that they've fully memorized the bar manual, but there is really only one way for the manager to be sure of their knowledge and that is through giving written tests. A simple, well rounded, half-hour test will indicate to the manager exactly how well the new bartenders have prepared themselves.

The sample test in the appendix consists of 180 questions. A score of at least 160 correct should be mandatory before a trainee is allowed to actually start work.

With regards to testing, a manager must remember that not all people are good at taking tests. A hard working trainee who shows good potential, yet fails the test, should be allowed to retake it one or two times.

The test should also be used as a training aid, by reviewing the mistakes with the trainee. This will actually serve as one last means of eliminating misunderstandings before the trainee actually starts working.

MOTIVATIONAL TECHNIQUES

After their preliminary training, bartenders, like all employees, should continually work to improve their skills. One of the best ways to insure this is by implementing an incentive program based on the bartender's rate of improvement. An example of such a program is outlined below.

Bartenders' Incentive Program

After successfully completing the initial training program, each bartender is placed on a one-month probation period and paid at the established probation period rate. After probation, if the bartender has worked in a satisfactory manner, the bartender is given a raise to the level of a starting bartender and, from that point, will be evaluated every 90 days for a ten percent raise, until the top bartender's wage has been reached. The probation period rate and the starting bartender rate should be dependent upon the individual bartender's experience.

It should be explained that all bartenders will be expected to continually work to improve their work habits, and that all bartenders will be expected to eventually make the top hourly wage. It should be emphasized that bartenders who refuse to improve and are content with performing at only a mediocre level will not only remain at their starting rate of pay, but will eventually be terminated. The goal is for each bartender and, as a result the entire liquor program, to continually improve.

After each evaluation, whether a raise was given or not, the bartender should be given specific goals to work toward. No bartender should feel satisfied until he or she has reached the top level of pay. Once this level has been reached, the bartender should not only be a complete professional, but an outstanding employee as well.

A successful bartender's hourly wage would progress as follows:

TIME	PERIOD	WAGE
1 Week	Training	Training Rate
30 Days	Probation	Probation Rate
90 Days	Starting	Base Rate
90 Days	First Raise	110% Base Rate
90 Days	Second Raise	120% Base Rate
	Final Raise	130% Base Rate

Further raises are based on time and the bartender's ability to maintain a level of excellence. Evaluation is made for these raises every 180 days.

To complement the 90 day personal evaluations, group bartender meetings should be scheduled at least three times per year.

Group Meetings

The purpose of bartender meetings is to stimulate motivation and establish goals for the entire liquor program. The goals should be general, such as lowering the liquor cost, increasing the cleanliness of the bar, increasing sales, or increasing the use of proper etiquette.

In the meetings, all problems should be openly discussed and the manager should attempt to get all bartenders to think in terms of progress. For example, if the liquor cost is running 1 percent too high, the manager should present the problem to the bartenders. The bartenders might suggest increasing a few of the prices and tightening a few of the portioning policies. The object is for management to present the problem and get the bartenders to offer the solutions. This will have the result of the bartenders thinking in terms of progress.

Well organized group meetings have the effect of strengthening the lines of communication between the bartenders and management, and as a result can dramatically add to the success of the entire liquor program. The importance of good communication cannot be overemphasized. It's an absolutely critical phase of management. Scheduling group meetings is not simply a good idea, it's imperative!

Chapter 8

FOOD SERVERS

HIRING POLICIES

In hiring food servers, there needn't be much emphasis placed on an applicant's previous experience in serving wine or liquor. Experience is usually an asset, but if the applicant expresses a sincere willingness to study and learn, the skills required to work with either wine or cocktails can be acquired without extensive training.

JOB TRAINING

Each food server should be absolutely required to learn and always practice the proper techniques of selling wine and liquor, the proper etiquette involved in serving both wine and cocktails, and the house rules associated with working with the bartender.

With regard to wine and cocktails, food servers must become salespersons and not simply order takers. As good salespersons, they should have both a good understanding of their product and a good understanding of successful sales techniques.

What Food Servers Should Know about Liquor, Wine, and Beer

It's unrealistic to expect food servers to memorize the entire liquor inventory or to become connoisseurs of wine, but they should be knowledgeable enough to answer the most commonly asked questions. Specifically, they should be aware of the following:

1) The names of the bar's brands of well liquor
2) The brand of the house wine
3) The brand(s) of bottled beer
4) The brand(s) of draft beer
5) The brand(s) of light beer
6) The brand(s) of imported beer
7) The cost of a glass of wine
8) The cost of a half liter of wine
9) The cost of a full liter of wine
10) The number of glasses in a half liter and a full liter
11) At least two drinks to recommend
12) At least two after dinner drinks to recommend and describe
13) The names and descriptions of any specialty drinks
14) The most popularly requested red, white, and rose bottled wines
15) How many glasses in a half bottle and full bottle of wine
16) The proper pronunciation of the names of all bottled wines.

The need for training food servers in knowledge about bottled wines has long been a subject for argument. The assumption has been: "The more the food servers know about bottled wines, the more they'll sell." Unfortunately, this is not always the case. The great majority of food servers are not wine experts, and are not really interested in spending the time and effort studying to become wine experts. As a result, wine training programs are usually time consuming, costly, and unproductive.

A more realistic philosophy would be: "The more food servers know about how to sell bottled wines, the more bottled wines they'll sell."

There will be a percentage of customers who are knowledgeable wine drinkers, and if they happen to ask the food server for an opinion regarding the quality of a particular brand or vintage of wine, they'll be asking for either professional advice or an opinion based on experience. In such an instance, the food servers should reply only if they are qualified. They should never base their response on hearsay nor use a standard reply such as: "It is an excellent wine and would complement your meal nicely." It would be far more professional to turn the situation over to either the floor manager or a more qualified employee in an effort to offer the customers the knowledgeable response they deserve.

Successful Sales Techniques

Although much emphasis should be placed on food servers becoming salespersons, it should also be stressed that only a limited number of tactful suggestive sales techniques may be used. Customers should never be offended by a food server employing aggressive, "hard sell" methods of selling wine or cocktails.

The key to success in suggestive selling is consistency. Each food server must consistently suggest wine or cocktails at the following four intervals throughout the customer's meal:

When Greeting the Table

When greeting the table, each food server should introduce him- or herself and then inquire if the customer would care for a cocktail: *"Good evening, my name is John and I'll be serving you this evening. Would you care for a cocktail before your meal?"*

The food server should then stand quietly and *wait for a response* before inquiring about another beverage such as coffee or tea. The goal is to give the customer no other options, nothing else to think about, until they've made a decision on cocktails. The food server must patiently wait for the customer to say "no" before suggesting another beverage.

By greeting the table in this manner: *"Good evening, my name is John and I'll be serving you this evening. Would you care for a cocktail or a cup of coffee before your meal?"* the waiter would be giving the customer an alternative to cocktails by also suggesting coffee. Instead of simply making a yes or no decision on a cocktail, the customer is now deciding between a cocktail or coffee. As a result, many customers will order coffee and a great many liquor sales will be lost.

A rule to remember is that coffee always sells itself, cocktails don't. Customers who enjoy coffee will almost always order a cup at some point throughout the meal, whether they've ordered cocktails or not.

From the standpoint of cost, it's also far better for customers to order coffee at the end of the meal. At that point they'll usually only have one cup and possibly one refill, as opposed to ordering coffee immediately and having four or five refills.

Therefore, each time food servers greet a new table, they should, in order:

1) Pleasantly introduce themselves
2) Inquire *only* about cocktails
3) Wait for a response

After the First Cocktail Is Finished

It's important that the food server always inquire whether the customer would desire a second cocktail as soon as the first has been finished. As a rule, the great majority of customers who order one cocktail will desire a second, but may lose that desire if forced to wait for a long period of time.

The food server should be aware that most customers will be annoyed if they are not asked if they would enjoy another cocktail. Therefore, inquiring about a second cocktail is not only an excellent method of suggestive selling, but an important aspect of proper service as well.

The food server should also remember the specific type of cocktail the customer originally ordered. The customer will feel that the service is at a more professional level if asked, *"Would you care for another Martini?"* as opposed to *"Would you care for another cocktail?"* (and if the answer is yes) *"I'm sorry, what was it you were drinking?"*

After Taking the Entree Order

After taking the order for the entree, the food server should always ask the host if the party would care for wine with their meal. This should be asked regardless of whether the table had ordered cocktails or not.

At this point the food server must be prepared to answer a number of basic questions which will often be asked, such as:

"What is the brand of your house wine?"
"What is the price of a half liter of wine?"
"How many glasses does a liter contain?"
"Would you suggest a half bottle of wine or a full bottle?"
"A white wine sounds good, what would you suggest?"

When asked to suggest a particular type of red, white, or rose wine, the food server should simply inform the customer of the most popularly requested brand. For the customer who has no idea of what type of wine to order, the food server should simply quote the old rule of red wine with dark meat, white wine with fish or light colored meat, and rose as a compromise. For example, if a customer has ordered steak, the food server would simply recommend the most popular brand of red wine and suggest an appropriate size: *"Red wine is traditionally ordered with red meat. Our most popular request is Cabernet Sauvignon and since there are only two of you, I would suggest a half bottle."*

Prompt answers for these questions will usually result in a sale, while the "I'm not sure, but I'll find out" response will often result in the "That's okay, I think we'll skip wine tonight" reply. That is why it is imperative that food servers are trained to be able to quickly answer all of the most commonly asked questions about wine.

Very detailed questions are another matter. The more sophisticated wine drinker will either order wine automatically or ask detailed questions before making a decision. In such an instance, if the food server is not fully qualified to answer the questions, the most experienced member of the staff should be brought to the table. Such customers will enjoy an experienced opinion and usually respond by ordering a bottle of wine.

After the Meal

After the meal, the food server should not only inquire about dessert, but after dinner drinks as well. After dinner drinks can sell very well, but many customers are not familiar with them and may ask for suggestions. For this reason, each food server should be aware of at least two after dinner drinks to suggest and describe upon request.

When asked for a suggestion, the food server might respond as follows: *"A fine liqueur such as Grand Marnier or Amaretto is an excellent after dinner drink, either by itself or with coffee. If you enjoy a mild drink, I'd suggest a Grasshopper. It has a creamy, minty flavor."*

Wine Service Etiquette

Consistency within the area of service etiquette should be absolutely mandatory, especially in the serving of wine. Wine lovers find it particularly distasteful if their bottle of wine is not properly presented, opened, and poured.

Special care with wine service is an excellent means of impressing customers as to the professionalism not only of the food server, but of the establishment as a whole. Unfortunately, poor service in this area will have just the opposite effect. Therefore, this is one area of training which cannot be overemphasized.

In teaching proper serving etiquette, it's best to point out the equal importance of the three stages: the presentation, the uncorking, and the actual pouring.

The Presentation

The food server should arrive at the table fully prepared. This would include bringing the requested bottle, an opener that the server is familiar and adept with, a clean cloth napkin, and an ice bucket if a chilled wine is to be served. If the table settings do not include wine glasses, the server should be sure that the appropriate glasses are brought to the table before or with the wine. Once set in place at the table, these glasses should not be touched again by the server.

A red wine should be presented with a clean cloth napkin held underneath the bottle. A chilled wine should be presented in a similar manner, but should be brought to the table in an ice bucket, and the cloth napkin should first be used to dry the bottle. The ice bucket should always be set to the right of the host.

The presentation is performed by holding the bottle toward the guest who ordered the wine with the label facing uppermost and readily seen, and confirming the selection by announcing the size of the bottle and the variety, vineyard, and vintage (when appropriate) of the wine. An example of such an announcement would be, "A tenth of Pinot Noir by Robert Mondavi, 1977 vintage."

A point to stress regarding the presentation would be the proper pronunciation of both the wine and the vineyard. If unsure of either, the food server should ask either the manager or the bartender before approaching the table.

The presentation may seem to the food server to be a time-consuming inconvenience, so the manager should emphasize that it's an important ritual that not only assures the server that the correct wine has been brought to the table, but also shows courtesy to the guest, and adds atmosphere to the meal.

Uncorking the Wine

The uncorking should always be done at the table and within the view of all guests. The top portion of the seal should be removed by slicing it with a knife just under the lip of the bottle. The removed portion should then be discarded and the lip of the bottle should be cleaned of any residue with a cloth napkin.

The bottle is now prepared to be uncorked, which brings us to the question of the wine opener. Inexperienced servers may prefer, and should be allowed to use, the "butterfly" style of opener because it is easier to keep centered and requires less strength to remove the cork. On the other hand, experienced food servers usually prefer the more professional and more traditional lever style of opener because it's equipped with its own knife and is so small and lightweight that it can comfortably be concealed in a pocket. Either style of opener should be acceptable.

The actual removal of the cork should be done as gracefully as possible. If the food server has difficulty with the removal of the cork, he or she should leave the bottle at the table and seek the assistance of the floor manager. The bottle should never leave the table and be returned with the cork removed.

An experienced wine drinker will be able to determine whether the wine has been properly stored by smelling and examining the texture of the cork. Therefore, after the cork has been removed it should be presented to the person who ordered the wine by placing it within their easy reach.

Again the cloth napkin should be used to remove any cork fragments or added residue from the lip of the bottle.

The point to emphasize with the uncorking of the wine is the actual mechanics involved with the removal of the cork. If the corkscrew is inserted at an angle, or if it's inserted too deep or too shallow the cork may either break or crumble into the wine.

Pouring the Wine

Before the wine can be served, it must first be sampled and approved by the person who ordered it. This is done by pouring approximately one ounce of wine into his or her glass and waiting for approval. If the wine is satisfactory, the server should then proceed to the right and move around the table in a counterclockwise direction, filling each glass and finishing with the host's glass. The bottle should then be placed to the right of the host.

In training food servers it should be emphasized that wine glasses should never be filled to capacity. Depending on the size of the glass, each glass should never be more than one half to two thirds full. This will give the guest the opportunity to enjoy the aroma of the wine concentrated within the glass.

Also, while pouring, the bottle should be held only in the right hand, with the label facing outward, and it should always be brought to the properly placed glass. Again, the food server should never handle the glass.

Finally, after pouring each glass, the bottle should be slightly turned to distribute the last drop of wine on the lip of the bottle and thus prevent any dripping.

Serving Sparkling Wines

Champagne, or any sparkling wine, should be served in a manner very similar to white wines, with a few exceptions in the procedures of uncorking and pouring.

As with white wine, champagne should be brought to the table in an ice bucket and placed to the right of the host. The unopened bottle should be dried and then presented to the guest who ordered it. The bottle should be returned to the bucket until it's ready to be opened and served.

Because of the pressure within a bottle of champagne, removing the cork can be dangerous and a few precautionary steps must be taken. The bottle should always be handled gently. The server should remove the foil to just below the safety wire. A folded napkin should be held securely and completely across the top of the bottle while the server loosens the wire safety from underneath. After the safety wire has been loosened, the server should take care to point the bottle away from guests and should always keep one hand over the cork for protection in the event that the cork pops out by itself. The server should then hold the cork firmly with the napkin in the right hand and tilt the bottle to a 45-degree angle, while gently twisting the bottle with the left hand until the cork is eased out. The bottle should still be kept at the 45-degree angle for an additional five to ten seconds to help prevent any of the champagne from foaming out. The protective napkin can then be removed, the lip of the bottle cleaned, and the champagne sampled and approved by the guest.

Because champagne foams or bubbles while being poured, each glass will have to be poured in two motions, allowing the foam to settle down between pours. Care should be taken to pour gently and slowly to prevent the champagne from bubbling over the top of the glass.

When teaching champagne, or sparkling wine, service, it should be emphasized that the presentation, sampling and counterclockwise procedure of pouring is identical to that of serving a white wine. It should also be stressed that there does exist a real danger if the cork is not well secured.

Serving House Wines

House wines are usually served either by the glass, half liter, or full liter. The serving technique need not be as formal as that associated with bottled wines. The presentation and sampling can be eliminated, but the food server should still remember to never touch the wine glasses while pouring, never fill the glasses to capacity, and always leave the remainder of wine to the right of the host.

Cocktail Service Etiquette

Serving cocktails does not involve the formality of wine service, but does require the following rules of proper etiquette.

First, each cocktail served should always be served from a cocktail tray and always with a fresh cocktail napkin. Cocktails should be placed on the outside upper right-hand corner of the place setting. When serving cocktails, the food servers must be careful to never place their fingers on the lip of the glass.

Bottled beers should always be served with a fresh chilled glass and the glass should always be filled at the table. The empty beer bottle should be removed as soon as possible and additional beer should be served with a fresh chilled glass.

Empty cocktail glasses should be removed promptly, and again the food servers must be careful not to place their fingers into, or on the lip of the glass.

In teaching cocktail service etiquette, the manager should emphasize the importance of the garnish. It should be stressed that garnishes can dramatically affect the taste of a cocktail, so each food server must be very careful to listen closely while taking a cocktail order. If no garnish is specified, the cocktail must be garnished in the traditional manner.

Working with the Bartender

It's very important for the food servers to learn to work with the bartender in a smooth, efficient manner. Confusion in this area will not only be time consuming for both the bartender and the food server, but will be costly for the establishment as well.

For this reason it's imperative for the manager to establish firm rules on bar service station and make the bartender responsible for seeing that those rules are enforced.

Placing the Order

The quickest way for a food server to place a cocktail order is to simply call the order out loud to the bartender. This system is fast and could work efficiently if all the food servers and cocktail servers used exactly the same abbreviations and called their orders in basically the same order. Unfortunately, when dealing with a large number of food and cocktail servers there is usually a constant battle to maintain consistency. Hurried food servers have a reputation for calling drinks out of order and using strange abbreviations, which almost always lead to mistakes and friction with the bartender.

A better system is to have food servers simply print their cocktail orders on the back of their checks and place their check in an upright position facing the bartender. The bartender can then simply read the order and prepare the cocktails, in a manner similar to that of a cook.

This system is easier to manage because the checks can be audited daily and mistakes can be corrected immediately. Another advantage is that the food servers are free to leave the bar after placing the order. Otherwise, they'd have to patiently wait until the bartender is ready for them to call out their order and then answer any further questions the bartender might have.

Consistency in check writing must be emphasized in teaching this system. Each check must be written in exactly the correct manner, using correct abbreviations for the names of the cocktails and the methods of preparation.

Abbreviations used by food servers and bartenders appeared in the sample bar manual in the previous chapter.

There should also be rules pertaining to the actual writing format:

1) A diagonal line should always be written between the liquor and the mix. For example, a vodka and tonic would be written V/T.

2) Specific garnishes should be written in parentheses after the cocktail. For example, a Scotch and soda with a lemon twist would be written Sc/S (twist).

3) A horizontal line should be drawn between each order to prevent confusion. For example, if a party of two were to first order two bourbon and waters and then were to order a second round of one bourbon and water and one Margarita, the orders would be written as follows:

<u>   2 B/W   </u>
1 B/W
1 Maggie

4) If the exact same order were to be ordered again, the line should be drawn and the word "reorder" printed underneath it.

5) All orders should be printed, not written in script.

6) All orders should be written downward as opposed to across the check. For example, one vodka and tonic, one gin and tonic, and one Scotch and water should be written as follows:

1 V/T
1 G/T   not like this: 1 V/T, 1 G/T, 1 Sc/W
1 Sc/W

After the check has been written, the question arises of whether the food server should figure the price to aid the bartender. This is a policy which normally leads to far more mistakes and confusion than it does time saving. It's best to have the food servers center their attention on correctly writing the order, garnishing and serving the cocktails, and leave the pricing to the bartender.

Garnishing Cocktails

Each food server should be shown, in detail, how each garnish is to be served. They should know exactly how lemon twists and lime squeezes are served, how orange slices, pineapple spears, and lime wheels are properly placed, how flags are prepared, and how olives and onions are picked and served. With regard to garnishes, this is all servers should be required to memorize. Instead of antagonizing the food servers by forcing them to memorize a long list of garnishes, it's far better to post an alphabetically arranged list of cocktails and their proper garnishes at the bar service station. An example of such a list is shown in Figure 41.

After placing the order, food servers can simply check the list and prepare their garnishes. Besides saving time, this policy guarantees that all of the cocktails are prepared properly.

General Service Station Rules

Finally, to insure organization, a list of general service station rules regarding the handling of checks and the general conduct of the food servers should be posted.

A good method of handling the checks is through the use of two check holders, one located on each side of the service station. The holder on the bartender's right should be used for the new orders and the holder on the bartender's left should be used for completed orders.

When placing an order, the food server simply places the check, standing upright with the order facing the bartender, on the *"in"* check holder. After the order has been completed, the bartender rings the total on the check and places the check sideways in the *"out"* check holder.

There should also be a specific method of handling dirty glasses. The glasses should first be completely emptied and then returned to a designated area of the service station.

As far as conduct is concerned, it's best for the food servers to remain quiet while in the service station. By conversing with the bartender, customers at the bar, or even among themselves, food servers will normally be distracted from their jobs and make mistakes.

The real key to having an efficiently operating service station will always be the conduct of the bartender. The bartender must be both a police officer, in always enforcing the rules, and a teacher, in aiding new employees and answering questions for old employees. Bickering and arguing between the bartender and the food servers should never be allowed.

GARNISHES

Banana Amaretto	banana wheel, 2 short straws, nutmeg
Banana Daiquiri	banana wheel, 2 long straws
Black Russian	swizzle stick
Bloody Mary	lime squeeze, celery stick, cucumber wheel
Bloody Bull	lime squeeze, celery stick, cucumber wheel
Brandy Alexander	2 short straws, nutmeg
Bull Shot	lime squeeze, swizzle stick
Chi Chi	pineapple spear, red cherry, umbrella, 2 long straws
Cuba Libre	lime squeeze, swizzle stick
Daiquiri	2 short straws
Dirty Mudder	swizzle stick
Dirty White Mudder	swizzle stick
Dubonnet Cocktail	twist (swizzle stick if on the rocks)
Frozen Daiquiri	red cherry, 2 short straws
Gibson	onion (swizzle stick if on the rocks)
Gimlet	lime wheel, green cherry (swizzle stick if on the rocks)
Gin and tonic	lime squeeze, swizzle stick
Golden Cadillac	2 short straws
Golden Dream	2 short straws
Grasshopper	2 short straws
Greyhound	swizzle stick
Harvey Wallbanger	orange, 2 long straws
Island Breeze	pineapple spear, red cherry, umbrella, 2 long straws
John Collins	lime squeeze, red cherry, orange, 2 long straws
Mai Tai	pineapple spear, red cherry, umbrella, 2 long straws
Manhattan	red cherry (swizzle stick if on the rocks)
Dry	olive (swizzle stick if on the rocks)
Perfect	olive (swizzle stick if on the rocks)
Margarita	lime wheel, 2 short straws
Martini	olive (swizzle stick if on the rocks)
Melon Margarita	lime wheel, melon stick, 2 short straws
Mist	twist, swizzle stick
Old-Fashioned	twist, orange, red cherry and swizzle stick
Peach Daiquiri	mint sprig, 2 long straws
Pina Colada	pineapple spear, red cherry, umbrella, 2 long straws
Pink Lady	2 long straws
Pink Squirrel	2 short straws
Press (Presbyterian)	twist, swizzle stick

FIGURE 41

Printed Training Material

The study material that the food servers should be issued should be complete, but does not need to be a book within itself. Management should strive to produce an easy-to-read outline of only the major points covered during the training program, as covered in this chapter.

The guide should contain step-by-step instructions on suggesting cocktails; ordering cocktails from the bartender, including a list of abbreviations and proper conduct in the service station; instructions on serving etiquette for wine, sparkling wine, and cocktails; house guidelines on what to memorize—i.e., brand names of well liquor, brand and types of house wine and in what form it is available, along with information on the number of glasses to a liter and half liter; names and pronunciation of bottled wines available if the list is small enough to make this listing practical; and the names of the draft beer, light beer, and bottled beers available.

Testing

The written test for food servers does not have to be nearly as detailed as the test given to bartenders. The sample test in the Appendix has 48 questions; a score of at least 40 correct would be required before allowing a food server to start working with cocktails. The correct answers to the test would of course vary with the establishment.

MOTIVATIONAL TECHNIQUES

Group Meetings

At least once a year, a bar-oriented group meeting should be held for the entire staff of food servers. Besides emphasizing the importance of proper service etiquette, reviewing sales techniques, and discussing problem areas, the manager should describe from a business aspect, the importance of increasing liquor sales.

A dramatic illustration would be comparing the sale of a cup of coffee to the sale of a simple well drink, such as a bourbon and water. To more graphically illustrate the point, the manager should use either a chalk board or a poster board to diagram the chart illustrated below.

	BOURBON AND WATER	CUP OF COFFEE
SALES		
PRICE	$1.50	.40¢
COST	.16 —first ounce	.08 — first cup
	+ .04 —¼ ounce	+ .08 — second cup
	.20¢	+ .02 — ¼ cup
		+ .04 — cream and sugar
		.22¢
PROFIT	$1.30	.27¢

The cost of the bourbon and water is based on a 1¼-oz. portion of bourbon at a cost of $.16 per ounce. The cost of the coffee is based on the fact that the average person who orders a cup of coffee will have 1¼ refills and use four cents worth of cream and sugar.

Then, by simply subtracting the costs from the sales price the manager can derive an actual profit for each item.

This illustration often opens the eyes of food servers who had never before viewed liquor sales from a business standpoint. By seeing that one cocktail will yield almost the same profit as five cups of coffee, food servers will better realize the necessity of always suggesting cocktails.

Liquor Sales Contests

A simple means of increasing liquor sales is by initiating a liquor sales contest among the food servers. Such contests not only stimulate liquor sales, but usually have a positive effect on employee morale as well.

An unusual but profitable idea would be to hold liquor contests each month. Each month the format and the prizes could be changed to maintain employee interest. Such a program would result in the food servers continually thinking about and talking about liquor sales.

Only management should be involved in the actual running of the contest. The results should be posted daily and in a conspicuous location, such as the employee eating area.

The contests can be based on a number of different formats. For example, if bottled wine sales happen to be dropping, management might decide to hold a contest on the number of bottled wines sold. Such a contest would not hinder cocktail sales, but it would almost guarantee that food servers would never forget to enthusiastically ask their guests if they'd care for wine after taking the entree order. The resulting increase in wine sales should cover far more than the cost of the prizes and the cost of the time involved in running the contest.

A contest based on the number of after dinner drinks sold should enjoy the same success. It would not detract from other cocktail or wine sales, but it would ensure that each food server would always inquire as to whether his or her guests would care for after dinner drinks after their meal.

Simplifying the Steps in Obtaining Cocktails

The most common excuse food servers use for not selling more cocktails is the extra time involved. Often food servers will complain "selling cocktails involves too much extra work," or "the bartender is slow and hard to work with," or "the bar is crowded and too far away."

Unfortunately, these excuses are usually legitimate. Management must continually work to make cocktail service as easy for the food server as possible. The following steps will help alleviate this problem:

1) A firm rule that bartenders will be responsible for serving food servers as quickly as possible should be established.
2) Bartenders should help in garnishing all cocktails, when possible.
3) Food servers should not be required to memorize either cocktail prices or garnishes.
4) If the bartender is too busy to garnish the cocktails, there should be a posted list of the proper garnishes that the food servers can refer to in the service station.
5) Food servers should be allowed to leave the service station after placing their orders.
6) Bartenders should always play the role of teachers and help food servers, not intimidate them. Arguing or bickering with the food servers should never be allowed.

7) If possible, a service bar located close to the dining room should be operated exclusively for food servers.

Implementing these rules will solve many problems for the food servers by greatly reducing their responsibilities. Under such circumstances the food servers will have no excuse for not selling liquor or not writing their orders correctly.

The only problem that such a program might produce will be that bartenders will resent their added responsibilities. Fortunately, this problem can be easily rectified by simply increasing their wages. If the bartenders properly assume their roles of both teachers and helpers, the cost of their increase in pay will be very minor compared to the large increase in liquor sales.

Chapter 9

COCKTAIL SERVERS

HIRING POLICIES

In general, when hiring cocktail servers, most managers place too much emphasis on appearance and too little on ability.

As a rule, a skillful cocktail server will normally sell 15 to 20 percent more cocktails than one who is only moderately skilled. Over a period of a month, depending on the business, this can easily add up to a substantial amount.

Because sales are so dependent upon the skill of the cocktail server, experience is a valuable asset, especially in a busy bar or restaurant. Hiring trainees is not out of the question, but can be very costly if not handled properly.

Hiring Inexperienced Cocktail Servers

Experienced cocktail servers are seldom content working the slower shifts. For this reason it's a good practice to fill these shifts with trainees. Because the value of a cocktail server's experience is directly dependent upon the volume of business, hiring trainees for the slowest shifts will not result in a substantial loss in sales. In fact, the value of the experience they'll gain will far overshadow the cost of any loss in sales.

In hiring trainees, the manager should seek applicants who are responsible, very eager to learn, and adept at working with numbers and handling money.

The trainees will have to be responsible persons because they'll be dealing directly with customers, and will at times be solely responsible for seeing that house policies and, more importantly, state laws are adhered to. They will also be dealing with intoxicated customers who will at times present problems which the cocktail server will have to be mature and responsible enough to cope with.

They will have to be eager to learn because they'll be given material that they will have to memorize in detail. Cocktail servers will have to be much more adept at working with cocktails than are food servers and as a result will have to memorize both cocktail prices and garnishes.

They will have to be proficient at working with numbers because they will be continually adding the costs of a number of cocktails in their head, and finally, they will also have to be skillful cashiers because they will be collecting money and returning change throughout their shift. If a cocktail server is slow in either of these areas, his or her efficiency will be considerably lower—a situation costly to the establishment.

Hiring Experienced Cocktail Servers

In hiring experienced cocktail servers, the manager should evaluate applicants bearing in mind the same concerns as used in hiring experienced bartenders. The manager must first be assured that applicants are fully open to learning rules and responsibilities that they may not be familiar with. As a result, they must be open to possibly changing work habits that they've felt comfortable with for a considerable length of time.

If the applicant seems honestly agreeable to these first qualifications, the manager must then evaluate the applicant's work history. As with bartenders, the factors of quality of employment, stability of employment, and length of experience should be well examined.

JOB TRAINING

Training for cocktail servers can be categorized into four areas:
1) the check and cash control system
2) the bar operation
3) selling cocktails
4) secondary responsibilities

The Check and Cash Control System

It's imperative that managers implement a detailed system for the cocktail servers to obtain cocktails from the bar and collect cash from the customers. The system must be efficient, to aid the speed of the cocktail server; simple, to avoid confusion and mistakes; and secure, to control both customer and employee theft. Such systems are called "check and cash control systems."

When training new cocktail servers, the established check and cash control system must be emphasized and taught in detail.

An example of such a system is the traditional "cash and carry" system, which basically operates as follows:

1) The cocktail server takes the order from the customer and obtains the order from the bartender.

2) The bartender rings the total cost of the order on the cocktail server's check.

3) The cocktail server serves the cocktails and immediately collects the money from the customer. The server carries a bank from which change can be made.

4) The cocktail server will hold the money until the end of the shift. At that time, the server will add all of the charges on his or her checks and pay that total to the bartender.

As the name implies, the cocktail server will collect *cash* and *carry* the cash until it's finally paid to the bartender. The system is simple, but can lead to confusion and a large number of mistakes if management does not enforce detailed rules regarding the problem areas. Specifically, what if the customer wants to run a tab? What if the customer decides to pay by credit card? What if, by mistake, the cocktail server has an order rung on the wrong check? What if the customer decides to eat and would like to have the cocktail charges transferred to the food check? What if, after returning with an order, the cocktail server finds the customer has left? What if a customer sitting at the bar moves to a table in the lounge and takes the bartender's check?

These are only a few of the questions a manager will be continually faced with if a complete check and cash control system has not been established and taught in detail to both the bartenders and cocktail servers.

An example of a fully detailed system is outlined in the following.

A Check and Cash Control System Outline

1) Each cocktail server will obtain a $20.00 change bank and a stack of checks from the manager before starting the shift. The server will assume responsibility for both the checks and the bank by signing a ledger in the manager's office.

2) The server will date and initial each check before it is used.

3) On the first check the server will print the word "master," and use that check until it is completely full.

4) Each time a cocktail server obtains an order from the bartender the value of the order will be rung on the BRSV (bar service) key on the server's check. *No drinks can be served until their value is first rung on the cocktail server's check.*

5) The server will collect for each round of drinks immediately after the drinks are served. Change can be made through the server's bank, and larger bills can be broken through the bartender. The server will hold all of the money until the end of the shift.

6) If a guest wishes to run a tab (pay for the entire bill when leaving, as opposed to paying round by round) a separate check will be used exclusively for that table. On the top of the new check the server should write the table number at which that guest is sitting.

7) If the guest informs the cocktail server of his or her desire to run a tab after the drinks have already been rung on the server's "master" check, the server will have to transfer the value of the drinks from the master check to a new blank check.

This transfer will be done in writing, by completing each of the following four steps:

(1) Circle the incorrect ring
(2) Print directly under the circle the correct ring (unless the entire charge is to be transferred).
(3) Print to the left of the circle the amount to be transferred and the number of the check to which it will be transferred to.
(4) On the new check print the amount of the charge which was transferred and the number of the check it was transferred from.

An example of the procedure is illustrated in Figure 42. After the cocktail

TRANSFERRING FROM MASTER CHECK
TO BLANK CHECK

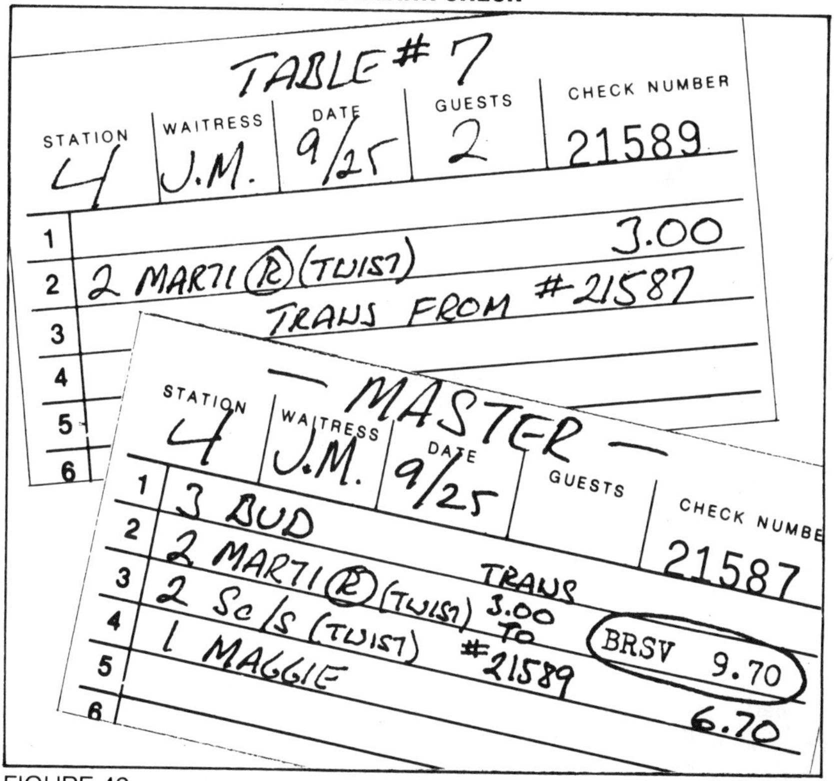

FIGURE 42

server had ordered drinks for three tables, the table ordering the two martini rocks ($3.00) decided to run a tab. The cocktail server then transferred the $3.00 off the master check and onto a blank check.

8) Charges which are transferred between checks of separate employees (i.e. from a bartender's check to a cocktail server's check) must be initialed by both employees on both checks.

9) The bartender's checks can never leave the bar. Therefore, if a customer sitting at the bar desires to move to a table in the cocktail lounge, the bartender will have to transfer that customer's charges to the cocktail server's check. The cocktail server would then be responsible for the entire bill.

10) No charge will be allowed to be transferred from the bar or cocktail lounge into the dining room.

CHECK SLIP

```
                        Starting #                    Ending #

Used Checks:  _____     _____
Unused Checks: _____    _____
Missing Checks:

_____  _____  _____

_____  _____  _____

Signature:  _____
Date:  _____  Shift:  _____
```

FIGURE 43

11) All over-rings must be circled and initialed by the bartender. Over-rings should never be scratched out or future ring-ups adjusted to compensate for previous over-rings.

12) When customers pay by credit card, the credit card slip should be immediately turned in to the bartender and exchanged for money.

13) If the cocktail server finds that customers have left after ordering their drinks, the server should immediately return the full drinks to the bartender. The bartender will then print the words "walk out" on the server's check and treat the charge as an over-ring.

14) After the shift, the cocktail servers should place all of their checks in numerical order and then use an adding machine to determine the total amount of all of the ring-ups.

15) The total amount should then be paid to the bartender who will ring that total, on the SVPD (service paid) key, onto the cocktail server's last check.

16) The server should then fill out a check slip, as illustrated in Figure 43.

17) The cocktail server should then bundle the used checks, unused checks, adding machine tape, and the check slip together and turn them, along with the $20.00 change bank, back to the manager. The manager will then initial the ledger to signify that everything has been returned satisfactorily.

There are a large number of check and cash control systems, but the successful systems have the following two factors in common:

1) **Nothing leaves the bar without being accounted for.** There are a number of ways of doing this, besides equipping the bar cash register with a bar service key, as was illustrated in the previous example.

To increase the speed of the bartender, some bars use the "red line system," in which the servers write out and fully price each order and the bartender simply draws a red line under the order to signify that the cocktails were indeed prepared and served.

Other bars have gone to computers, and the servers are taught to log each order into the computer before placing it with the bartender. The bartenders are then instructed never to prepare orders which have not been printed by the computer documentor.

What each of these systems has in common is that all of the drinks served have been accounted for.

2) **All checks are counted and each transaction is audited by management daily.** The fundamental principle in check controls is that every check be accounted for *daily* and that every transaction on every check be audited *daily*. How strict management is within this area will directly determine how successful the check and cash control system will be.

The Bar Operation

To work efficiently, cocktail servers will have to thoroughly familiarize themselves with the following four areas:

Garnishes. Even though a garnish list may be posted at the liquor service station, it would be far too time-consuming for the cocktail server to have to continually refer to it. Cocktail servers should be required to memorize the proper garnish for each cocktail.

Prices. By memorizing all of the liquor prices, cocktail servers will not only eliminate a huge number of mistakes, but also aid the efficiency of the bartender. Cocktail servers should be responsible for listing the correct price for each order on the right hand side of the check. This will save the bartender the time required to determine the cost of each round.

Service station rules. Cocktail servers should use exactly the same methods of ordering cocktails as food servers use. They should use the same abbreviations and write their orders in exactly the same manner.

In an effort to reduce confusion and mistakes, management must insist on consistency within this area.

Call liquor. Besides having to memorize the various brands of beer, well liquor, and house wines, cocktail servers should also know the various brands of call liquor stocked by the bar. This way they will be able to immediately answer customer questions and immediately correct customers who order brands of liquor the bar does not offer. This knowledge will save the cocktail server needless trips to the bar and add to the general efficiency of the cocktail lounge.

Secondary Responsibilities

In order to keep the cocktail lounge clean and the bar service station continually well stocked, management will have to assign to the cocktail server definite cleaning and stocking responsibilities, similar to those assigned to the bartenders.

When training, management should stress that these secondary responsibilities will be enforced just as stringently as those rules associated with the check and cash control system.

One of the best ways of enforcing the rules pertaining to the cocktail servers side work is to simply post a list of the side work responsibilities somewhere in the bar service station and make it a rule that all cocktail servers refer to that list daily. An example of such a list follows:

Cocktail Server's Side Work

Immediately Upon Arrival

1) Check to see that each table in your station has:
   a) A cleanly wiped surface
   b) Two ashtrays
   c) A clean table tent
   d) A lit candle
2) Check to see that all of the chairs in your station are cleanly wiped and arranged properly.
3) Check the floor area and call a busboy if it needs to be swept.

Throughout Your Shift

1) See that the bar service station stays stocked with:
   a) Cocktail napkins

b) Cocktail straws and stir sticks

c) Clean cocktail trays

d) Ashtrays

e) Clean towels

f) Fresh coffee

g) Hot water

After Your Shift

1) Wipe clean and properly organize all of the tables and chairs in your station.

2) Blow out all of the candles.

3) Clean or replace any dirty or torn table tents.

4) Send the dirty ashtrays to the dishwasher.

5) Send the dirty towels to the kitchen.

6) Pour out the remaining coffee and hot water and turn off the warmer.

7) Wipe off the cocktail trays.

8) Restock the service station with napkins, straws, and stir sticks.

Selling Cocktails

The job of a cocktail server is not to simply serve cocktails, but to *sell* cocktails. This is not to say that good cocktail servers are pushy or aggressive toward their customers, they are simply very proficient at *selling* cocktails through continually keeping a close eye on their tables and anticipating their customer's needs.

In training cocktail servers to increase their sales, the following routine should be emphasized:

1) Greet each new table immediately.

2) Many customers will ask for a suggestion; therefore always remember at least three cocktails to recommend.

3) Learn to minimize the number of trips to the bar by taking orders from several tables at one time.

4) Even when no one in your station needs your service, make yourself easily available by continually circulating through your tables and checking for dirty ashtrays and empty glasses.

5) Do not wait until each customer has completely finished his or her drink

before inquiring about another cocktail. Make your first inquiry when the customer is three quarters through with his or her drink.

6) Never spend too much time with one customer or with one table.

7) Dirty tables should be cleared and cleanly wiped down as soon as the customers leave the table.

8) While engaging in conversation with one customer, stay observant and be aware of the needs of other tables.

The Printed Training Material

The cocktail server's training guide should deal primarily with the highlights of the check and cash control system, and the areas of the bar operation that must be memorized (the prices, the garnishes, the call liquor inventory, and the ordering procedures).

The handout would consist of the same information on ordering cocktails from the bartender that the food servers use, listing abbreviations for well liquor, mixes, preparation methods, cocktails, beer, house wine, and call liquor, as well as information on placing the order. The check and cash control system as explained in this chapter should be explained in the printed training material. Garnishes and prices should be spelled out in detail.

The Written Test

The sample test located in the Appendix was designed to give the manager a clear understanding of a trainee's knowledge of the liquor program. The test is fair, but unless the trainee if fully prepared, he or she will find the test difficult.

The test consists of 150 questions, and management should make a score of at least 130 correct mandatory before allowing the trainees to start work.

MOTIVATIONAL TECHNIQUES

Group Meetings

Even though most managers are aware of the importance of group meetings, they have a tendency to overlook meetings with cocktail servers. They reason that cocktail servers perform only a limited number of duties and therefore, in an effort to save time, it's convenient to occasionally group them with bartenders and hold a general employee meeting rather than separate meetings for the cocktail servers. From the standpoint of employee motivation this is a definite mistake.

It's true that cocktail servers have only a limited number of responsibilities, but it's also true that cocktail servers play a very important role in determining the success of the cocktail lounge. Besides establishing good customer relations, a good cocktail server can also be extremely helpful in the promotion and operation of special events such as holiday promotions, televised sporting events, or the cocktail hour.

For this reason, it can be very rewarding for management to motivate cocktail servers by giving them the opportunity to both express their views regarding the operation of the cocktail lounge, and to actually participate in the organization of special events.

A manager who realizes the potential involved will make it a firm policy to hold group meetings with only the cocktail servers at least twice each year.

Salary Incentive

Traditionally, cocktail servers are hired at minimum wage and derive the remainder of their income from tips. From a business standpoint, this is a good policy, because besides holding the labor cost down it also inspires the servers to work harder for their tips.

Unfortunately, it has also become traditional to keep cocktail servers at minimum wage, with the manager explaining, "You'll make your own raises by working harder to develop a rapport with your customers and, in doing so, develop an increasingly large following of steady customers."

This is true, but it's also true that this increased following of steady customers will result in increased liquor sales for the establishment.

As a rule, the value of a good cocktail server is usually grossly underrated. Management usually considers only the limited amount of actual duties a cocktail server performs, and fails to realize the increased amount of sales which can be directly attributed to the work of a specific and skilled cocktail server.

Therefore, besides simply holding meetings with the cocktail servers, management should break down tradition and periodically evaluate each cocktail server's performance and, when appropriate, issue raises. A $0.25-per-hour raise to a full time cocktail server will only increase the net labor cost by $10.00 each week. Even in a moderately busy bar, a quality cocktail server can make up that amount in half a shift.

It's obvious that from the standpoint of cost such raises will affect the establishment very little, but from the standpoint of employee motivation they can have a very dramatic effect.

APPENDIX

BARTENDER'S TRAINING TEST

Name: _____

Date: _____

PART ONE: RECIPES

The first portion of the test deals with the preparation of cocktails. In answering each question use the abbreviations listed below.

Glassware

R   = Rock Glass   So = Sour Glass
H   = Highball Glass   St = Shot Glass
TH = Tall Highball Glass Sn = Snifter
B   = Bucket Glass   Sy = Sherry Glass
C   = Cocktail Glass   Cd = Cordial Glass
M   = Martini Glass   Cm = Champagne Glass
Mg = Margarita Glass

Garnishes

RC = Red Cherry   Or = Orange Slice
GC = Green Cherry   C   = Celery
O = Olive   P   = Pineapple Spear
On = Onion   St = Stir Stick
T = Twist   LS = Long Straw
L = Lime   SS = Short Straw
LW = Lime Wheel

Methods of Preparation

B   = Build   MG = Mixing Glass
BL = Blend   MC = Mixing Can

On the following chart answer each question in the same manner as the examples listed below. Each correct answer is worth one point.

	Glass	Method	Garnish	Ingredients
1) Martini Up	M	MG	O	2 oz. Gin, Dash of Dry Vermouth
2) Tom Collins	TH	B	RC, Or, L, 2 LS	1¼ oz. Gin, Fill remainder with half sweet sour and half lemon lime soda

RECIPES

	Glass	Method	Garnish	Ingredients
1) Manhattan Rocks				
2) Bloody Mary				
3) Tom Collins				
4) Pina Colada				
5) Black Russian				
6) Margarita				
7) Greyhound				
8) Mai Tai				
9) Gimlet Up				
10) Whiskey Sour				
11) Ramos Fizz				
12) Daiquiri				
13) Tequila Sunrise				
14) Singapore Sling				
15) Grasshopper				
16) Brandy Alexander				
17) Golden Cadillac				
18) Irish Coffee				
19) Old-Fashioned				
20) Rusty Nail				

PART TWO: PRICES

List the price of each of the drinks on the left hand column and list the price of a straight shot of each of the liquors on the right hand column.

21) Vodka Rocks	_____	50) Well Bourbon	_____
22) Scotch and Soda	_____	51) Jose Cuervo Gold	_____
23) John Collins	_____	52) Dry Sack	_____
24) Screwdriver	_____	53) Wild Turkey	_____
25) Martini Up	_____	54) Jack Daniel's	_____
26) Bloody Mary	_____	55) Crème de Menthe	_____
27) Black Russian	_____	56) Cutty Sark	_____
28) White Russian	_____	57) Grand Marnier	_____
29) Rusty Nail	_____	58) Myers Rum	_____
30) King Alphonse	_____	59) Beefeater	_____
31) Strawberry Daiquiri	_____	60) Kahlua	_____
32) Double Martini Rocks	_____	61) Ruby Port	_____
33) Golden Dream	_____	62) Dubonnet	_____
34) Harvey Wallbanger	_____	63) Tanqueray	_____
35) Gimlet Rocks	_____	64) Tia Maria	_____
36) Wine Cooler	_____	65) Bacardi Silver	_____
37) Plain Cola	_____	66) V.O.	_____
38) Glass of Rose	_____	67) Courvoisier	_____
39) ½ Liter of Burgundy	_____	68) Bombay	_____
40) Liter of Chablis	_____	69) Triple Sec	_____
41) Bottle of Michelob	_____	70) Galliano	_____
42) Bottle of Budweiser	_____	71) Crown Royal	_____
43) Bottle of Millers	_____	72) 151 Rum	_____
44) Cappuccino	_____	73) Old Overholt	_____
45) Irish Coffee	_____	74) Peppermint	
46) Hot Buttered Rum	_____	Schnapps	_____
47) Mai Tai	_____	75) Black Label	_____
48) Pina Colada	_____	76) Red Label	_____
49) Zombie	_____	77) 7 Crown	_____
		78) Smirnoff	_____

PART THREE: ABBREVIATIONS

List the proper abbreviations that the food and cocktail servers will be required to use for each of the following drinks:

79) Bourbon and water _____

80) Vodka and tonic _____

81) Gin on the rocks _____

82) Martini on the rocks _____

83) Manhattan up _____

84) Margarita _____

85) Bloody Mary _____

86) Screwdriver _____

87) Salty Dog _____

88) Black Russian _____

89) Plain soda _____

90) Glass of rosé _____

91) Half liter of burgundy _____

92) Liter of rosé _____

93) Bottle of Michelob _____

94) Draft beer _____

95) Jack Daniel's on the rocks _____

96) V.O. and water _____

97) Cutty Sark and soda _____

98) Grasshopper _____

99) Pina Colada _____

100) Old-Fashioned _____

PART FOUR: TRUE AND FALSE

101) Smoking is never allowed behind the bar. _____

102) Eating is allowed behind the bar only when the bartender is on break. _____

103) Each bartender is allowed to issue three complimentary drinks each day. _____

104) All highball drinks are prepared with 1¼ oz. of liquor. _____

105) Employees are allowed in the bar only after their shift and only when out of uniform. _____

106) Employees may never sit at the bar. _____

107) The opening bartender should check the liquor inventory daily. _____

108) Each glass must be dried and polished before being replaced on the backbar. _____

109) It's acceptable for the bartenders to use their hands in place of ice scoops as long as their hands are clean. _____

110) All liquor must be measured with a measuring glass (jigger or lined shot glass). _____

111) If possible, bartenders should always aid the food servers in garnishing cocktails. _____

112) Each drink should be served with a fresh napkin. _____

113) Serving obviously intoxicated customers is against the law. _____

114) It's very important that food servers are served as quickly as possible. _____

115) Bartenders may read newspapers or books while on duty if business is slow. _____

116) Bartenders will be held accountable for all of their bar checks.   _____

117) No employees other than bartenders are allowed behind the bar.   _____

118) All liqueurs are served in 1½ oz. portions.   _____

119) Vermouths may be free poured.   _____

120) Mistakes made on the cash register must be initialed by the bartender.   _____

Results

	Questions	Mistakes		Totals
PART I	80	– _____	=	_____
PART II	58	– _____	=	_____
PART III	22	– _____	=	_____
PART IV	20	– _____	=	_____
		TOTAL	=	_____

REVIEW

Date: _____

Manager: _____

Comments:

_____

_____

_____

_____

_____

Employee Signature: _____

THE COCKTAIL SERVERS TRAINING TEST

Name: _____

Date: _____

List the price, garnish and proper abbreviation for each of the items listed below. When listing the garnish, use the following abbreviations:

RC = Red Cherry   Or = Orange Slice
GC = Green Cherry   C = Celery
O = Olive   P = Pineapple
On = Onion   St = Stir Stick
T = Twist   LS = Long Straw
L = Lime   SS = Short Straw
LW = Lime Wheel   NG = No Garnish

Examples:

	PRICE	GARNISH	ABBREVIATION
1) Brandy on the rocks	$1.50	St	Bdy®
2) Tom Collins	1.50	L, Or, RC, 2LS	T. Collins

	PRICE	GARNISH	ABBREVIATION
1) Bourbon and water			
2) Vodka on the rocks			
3) Tall gin and tonic			
4) Margarita with no salt			
5) Glass of Rosé			
6) Old-Fashioned			
7) Black Label on the rocks			
8) Bottle of Budweiser			
9) Martini up with a twist			

	PRICE	GARNISH	ABBREVIATION
10) Tall Cutty Sark and soda			
11) Manhattan on the rocks			
12) Grand Marnier			
13) Dewar's White Label and water			
14) Draft beer			
15) Dry Sack up			
16) Pina Colada			
17) Half liter of chablis			
18) Myers Rum and Coke			
19) Mai Tai			
20) Jack Daniel's on the rocks			
21) Tequila Sunrise			
22) Bombay Martini up			
23) Bottle of Michelob			
24) Vodka Gimlet			
25) Chivas Regal on the rocks			
26) Liter of burgundy			
27) Virgin Mary			
28) Blackberry Brandy up			
29) Irish coffee			
30) Singapore Sling			

	PRICE	GARNISH	ABBREVIATION
31) Beefeater Martini up			
32) Golden Cadillac			
33) Black Russian			
34) Rob Roy on the rocks			
35) C.C. and Seven			
36) Tia Maria			
37) Gibson on the rocks			
38) Strawberry Daiquiri			
39) Tall Tanqueray and tonic			
40) Red Label and soda			
41) Bacardi and Coke			
42) Crown Royal and water			
43) Courvoisier			
44) Ramos Fizz			
45) Seven and Seven			
46) Drambuie			
47) Creme de Menthe on the rocks			
48) Harvey's Bristol Cream up			
49) Mexican coffee			
50) J&B and soda			

Results

TOTAL QUESTIONS: 150
— TOTAL MISTAKES: _____
TOTAL SCORE: _____

REVIEW

Date: _____

Manager: _____
Comments:

_____

_____

_____

_____

_____

Employee Signature: _____

THE FOOD SERVER'S TEST ON BAR POLICIES

Name: _____

Date: _____

PART ONE: FILL IN THE BLANKS

1) Our well bourbon is _____ .

2) Our well scotch is _____ .

3) Our well gin is _____ .

4) The brand of our house wine is _____ .

5) The three types of house wines are _____ ,
_____ , and _____ .

6) Our most popularly requested bottled red wine is
_____ .

7) Our most popularly requested bottled white wine is
_____ .

8) Our only draft beer is _____ .

9) We stock five types of bottled beers; they are
_____ , _____ ,
_____ , _____ , and
_____ .

10) Our only light beer is _____ .

PART TWO: ABBREVIATIONS

List the proper ordering abbreviations for each of the following:

11) Vodka on the rocks _____

12) Scotch and soda _____

13) Bourbon and Seven with a twist _____

14) Tall gin and tonic _____

15) Cutty Sark and water _____

16) V.O. and Seven-Up _____

17) Martini on the rocks with a twist _____

18) Manhattan up _____

19) Tom Collins _____

20) Margarita with no salt _____

21) Whiskey sour on and over _____

22) Bloody Mary _____

23) Tequila Sunrise _____

24) Glass of chablis _____

25) Half liter of burgundy _____

26) Bottle of Budweiser _____

27) Draft beer _____

28) Cola _____

29) Shirley Temple _____

PART THREE: TRUE OR FALSE

30) Red wine should always be served at room temperature.   _____

31) Each bottle of wine should be presented to the host (or person who ordered the wine) before being opened.   _____

32) After the cork has been removed from the bottle, it should immediately be discarded.   _____

33) Wine should always be poured with the right hand.   _____

34) Each glass should be filled to capacity.   _____

35) After each glass has been filled, the remainder of the wine should be placed to the right of the host.   _____

36) When removing the cork from a bottle of Champagne, the bottle should be held firmly with the left hand and should be standing upward.   _____

37) Opening a bottle of Champagne can be very dangerous, and the bottle should always be held facing away from all guests.   _____

38) After the cork has been removed, the bottle of Champagne should be held at a 45-degree angle for five to ten seconds.   _____

39) The food server is required to use a cocktail tray only when serving three or more cocktails.   _____

40) Each cocktail should be served with a fresh napkin.   _____

41) Cocktails should never be garnished unless requested so by the customer.   _____

42) Each bottle of beer should be served with a fresh chilled glass.   _____

Results

	Questions	Mistakes		Totals
PART I	16	– _____	=	_____
PART II	19	– _____	=	_____
PART III	13	– _____	=	_____
		TOTAL	=	_____

REVIEW

Date: _____

Manager: _____
Comments:

_____

_____

_____

_____

_____

Employee Signature: _____

GENERAL REVIEW

The following questions are related to general knowledge that a professional bartender should be aware of. All of the answers to the questions can be found in Chapter Five.

TEST ONE: VOCABULARY

The correct definition for each of the following words can be found listed in Chapter Five under "General Vocabulary." After you've defined *each word*, check that section to verify your accuracy.

1) Back   _____
2) Blended Whiskey   _____
3) Straight Whiskey   _____
4) Well Liquor   _____
5) Call Liquor   _____
6) Premium Call Liquor   _____
7) Liqueur   _____
8) Aperitif   _____
9) Double   _____
10) Draw   _____
11) Float   _____
12) Frappe   _____
13) Mist   _____
14) Proof   _____
15) Quinine   _____
16) Virgin   _____
17) Dry   _____
18) Over   _____
19) On and Over   _____
20) Up   _____

TEST TWO: BRAND NAMES

The brand names of a variety of liquors are listed on the left side of the page. Try to correctly identify what type of liquor each brand is. The answers are coded as follows:

SBW = Straight Bourbon Whiskey
BIW = Blended Whiskey
CW = Canadian Whisky
SW = Scotch Whisky
IW = Irish Whisky
RW = Rye Whiskey
V = Vodka
RV = Russian Vodka
G = Gin
T = Tequila
B = Brandy
JR = Jamaican Rum
PR = Puerto Rican Rum
Cg = Cognac
Lq = Liqueur
Cr = Cordial
AW = Aperitif Wine
SHY = Sherry

1) Jim Beam
2) Beefeater
3) 7 Crown
4) Courvoisier
5) Myers
6) Grand Marnier
7) Cutty Sark
8) V.O.
9) Christian Brothers
10) Dry Sack
11) Smirnoff
12) Wild Turkey
13) Bacardi
14) Kahlua
15) Tanqueray
16) José Cuervo
17) C. C. (Canadian Club)

1) _____
2) _____
3) _____
4) _____
5) _____
6) _____
7) _____
8) _____
9) _____
10) _____
11) _____
12) _____
13) _____
14) _____
15) _____
16) _____
17) _____

18) J&B	18) _____
19) Old Overholt	19) _____
20) Old Bushmills	20) _____
21) Amaretto	21) _____
22) Green Creme De Menthe	22) _____
23) Bombay	23) _____
24) Dewar's White Label	24) _____
25) Vandermint	25) _____
26) Ron Rico	26) _____
27) Ballantine's	27) _____
28) Hennessey	28) _____
29) Martell	29) _____
30) Crown Royal	30) _____
31) Harvey's Bristol Cream	31) _____
32) Galliano	32) _____
33) Stolichnaya	33) _____
34) Murphy's	34) _____
35) Johnnie Walker Black Label	35) _____
36) Tia Maria	36) _____
37) Chivas Regal	37) _____
38) Creme De Cassis	38) _____
39) Jack Daniels	39) _____
40) Ruby Port	40) _____
41) Drambuie	41) _____
42) Early Times	42) _____
43) Johnnie Walker Red Label	43) _____
44) Old Grand Dad	44) _____
45) E & J	45) _____
46) Bacardi 151	46) _____
47) Dubonnet	47) _____
48) Creme De Banana	48) _____
49) I.W. Harper	49) _____
50) Strega	50) _____

TEST THREE: GLASSWARE

A wide variety of drinks are listed on the left side of the page. Try to correctly identify the type of glass used to serve each drink.
The glassware is coded as follows:

R   =   Rock glass
H   =   Highball glass
TH =   Tall highball glass
M   =   Martini glass
Mg =   Margarita glass
C   =   Cocktail glass
B   =   Bucket glass
        (double Old-Fashioned glass)
Sn =   Snifter
St =   Shot glass
Cd =   Cordial glass
Sy =   Sherry glass
Cm =   Champagne glass
So =   Sour glass

1) Bourbon rocks   1) _____
2) Bourbon and water   2) _____
3) Tall bourbon and water   3) _____
4) Bloody Mary   4) _____
5) V.O. rocks   5) _____
6) Tom Collins   6) _____
7) Cutty and soda   7) _____
8) Margarita   8) _____
9) Courvoisier   9) _____
10) Pina Colada   10) _____
11) Dry Sack   11) _____
12) Martini   12) _____
13) Beefeater rocks   13) _____
14) Greyhound   14) _____
15) Tall Beam and water   15) _____
16) Black Russian   16) _____
17) Vodka and tonic   17) _____
18) Golden Cadillac   18) _____
19) Gin and tonic   19) _____
20) Mai Tai   20) _____
21) Grand Marnier   21) _____
22) Wine Cooler   22) _____

23) Hennessey	23) _____
24) Press	24) _____
25) Shot of Chivas Regal	25) _____
26) Brave Bull	26) _____
27) Manhattan on the rocks	27) _____
28) Gibson up	28) _____
29) Brandy and soda	29) _____
30) Gimlet up	30) _____
31) Cuba Libre	31) _____
32) Harvey Wallbanger	32) _____
33) Strawberry Margarita	33) _____
34) Singapore Sling	34) _____
35) Sour rocks	35) _____
36) Old-Fashioned	36) _____
37) Peppermint Schnapps	37) _____
38) Tequila Sunrise	38) _____
39) King Alphonse	39) _____
40) Whiskey Sour	40) _____
41) Vodka and Seven	41) _____
42) Screwdriver	42) _____
43) Scotch and soda	43) _____
44) Grasshopper	44) _____
45) Bacardi and Coke	45) _____
46) Rusty Nail	46) _____
47) Tuaca	47) _____
48) Ramos Fizz	48) _____
49) Brandy	49) _____
50) Bacardi cocktail	50) _____

TEST FOUR: GARNISHES

Try to identify the correct garnishes for the drinks listed on the left side of the page.
The garnishes are coded as follows:

RC	=	Red cherry
GC	=	Green cherry
O	=	Olive
On	=	Onion
T	=	Twist
L	=	Lime squeeze
LW	=	Lime wheel
Or	=	Orange slice
C	=	Celery
P	=	Pineapple spear
LS	=	Long straw
SS	=	Short straw
LS	=	Long straw
St	=	Stir (plastic or swizzle stick)

1) Bourbon rocks   1) _____
2) Bourbon and water   2) _____
3) Tall bourbon and water   3) _____
4) Tequila Sunrise   4) _____
5) Screwdriver   5) _____
6) Gin and tonic   6) _____
7) Mai Tai   7) _____
8) Press   8) _____
9) Tom Collins   9) _____
10) Martini   10) _____
11) Martini on the rocks   11) _____
12) V.O. and Seven   12) _____
13) Margarita   13) _____
14) Greyhound   14) _____
15) Tall Greyhound   15) _____
16) Black Russian   16) _____
17) Bloody Mary   17) _____
18) Rusty Nail   18) _____
19) Old-Fashioned   19) _____
20) Manhattan   20) _____
21) Ramos Fizz   21) _____
22) Cuba Libre   22) _____

23) Pina Colada	23) _____
24) Grasshopper	24) _____
25) Tall vodka and tonic	25) _____
26) Whiskey sour rocks	26) _____
27) Dry Rob Roy	27) _____
28) Perfect Manhattan rocks	28) _____
29) Dirty White Mudder	29) _____
30) Singapore Sling	30) _____
31) Gimlet	31) _____
32) Gimlet rocks	32) _____
33) Daiquiri	33) _____
34) Stinger up	34) _____
35) 7 and 7	35) _____
36) Chi Chi	36) _____
37) Pink Lady	37) _____
38) Spritzer	38) _____
39) Tanqueray and tonic	39) _____
40) V.O. Manhattan up	40) _____
41) Bombay martini rocks	41) _____
42) Stinger rocks	42) _____
43) Scotch rocks	43) _____
44) Tall Ballantine's and soda	44) _____
45) Harvey Wallbanger	45) _____
46) Dry brandy Manhattan rocks	46) _____
47) Shirley Temple	47) _____
48) White Russian	48) _____
49) Cutty rocks	49) _____
50) Golden Dream	50) _____

TEST FIVE: ABBREVIATED NAMES

Try to identify the correct abbreviation for each of the following cocktails. It's important that you memorize these abbreviations because they will be the names you'll hear most often when working as a bartender. In the questions below, unless specified "on the rocks," Martinis, Manhattans, and Rob Roys are normally understood to be "up." In bourbon orders, the word "bourbon" is often omitted by servers and is to be assumed by the bartender. This technique is used to abbreviate orders.

1) Manhattan up   1) _____
2) Brandy Manhattan up   2) _____
3) Dry brandy Manhattan up   3) _____
4) Dry brandy Manhattan on the rocks   4) _____
5) Screwdriver   5) _____
6) Scotch and soda   6) _____
7) Gin and tonic   7) _____
8) Harvey Wallbanger   8) _____
9) Margarita   9) _____
10) Seagram's 7 Crown and Seven-Up   10) _____
11) Presbyterian   11) _____
12) Black Russian   12) _____
13) Draft beer   13) _____
14) Singapore Sling   14) _____
15) Whiskey sour   15) _____
16) Bloody Mary   16) _____
17) Pina Colada   17) _____
18) Salty Dog   18) _____
19) Tanqueray Martini up   19) _____
20) Old-Fashioned   20) _____
21) Tequila Sunrise   21) _____
22) King Alphonse   22) _____
23) Grasshopper   23) _____
24) Rusty Nail   24) _____
25) Bourbon on the rocks   25) _____
26) Bourbon and Seven   26) _____
27) Tall bourbon and soda   27) _____
28) Cola   28) _____
29) Orange juice   29) _____
30) Shirley Temple   30) _____
31) Glass of burgundy   31) _____
32) Half liter of burgundy   32) _____

33) Glass of chablis   33) _____
34) Virgin Bloody Mary   34) _____
35) Golden Cadillac   35) _____
36) Jack Daniels on the rocks   36) _____
37) Beefeater Martini up   37) _____
38) Canadian Club and ginger ale   38) _____
39) Jose Cuervo and tonic   39) _____
40) Johnnie Walker Red Label and soda 40) _____
41) Dewar's White Label and water   41) _____
42) Jim Beam on the rocks   42) _____
43) 7 Crown on the rocks   43) _____
44) Cutty Sark and water   44) _____
45) Wild Turkey and water   45) _____

TEST SIX: MISCELLANEOUS QUESTIONS

The correct answers to each of the following questions can be found in Chapter Five. After you've answered *each question,* turn to the appropriate section of Chapter Five and verify your answer.

1) What is the difference between straight and blended whiskeys?

2) Name at least four areas in the bar that should be cleaned daily.

3) If you were preparing a frozen cocktail, what type of mixer would you use?

4) What are the two reasons for using a mixing glass?

5) What are the three general areas of barmanship?

6) What is the function of each of the three sinks in the bar?

7) Explain the service/service paid method of liquor control.

8) Name at least four basic rules pertaining to customer relations.

9) What is the difference between Puerto Rican rum and Jamaican rum?

10) Why are all brandys not Cognacs?

11) Why should you never use crushed ice in a mixing glass?

12) How would you prepare an extra sweet Manhattan?

13) When we speak of the other half of bartending, what are we referring to?

14) What is the difference between a Daiquiri and a Barcardi Cocktail?

15) Name five items you might find in the bar refrigerator.

16) Name five brands of straight bourbon whiskey.

17) Why do some customers order their cocktails tall?

18) Regarding customer control, what two things must a bartender never forget?

19) How do you serve a lemon twist?

20) What does "B and B" refer to?

21) What does "P.C." refer to?

22) Are most of the popular Scotch whiskies straight or blended?

23) Why should you use only crushed ice in the blender?

24) What are six types of mixes you might find in a mix gun?

25) What are the three general rules pertaining to "The other half of bartending"?

26) With regard to speed, what are the only two rules you must remember?

27) What are the six steps (in order) in which you should memorize each recipe?

28) What are the two ingredients in Collins mix?

29) What drink might be referred to as a "Scotch Manhattan"?

30) Why is it a bartender's job to be a good listener?

31) Name at least four rules of etiquette pertaining to preparing and serving cocktails.

32) Name ten different types of glassware.

33) Why is a strainer not used with a blender?

34) What is the difference between a Harvey Wallbanger and a Tall Screwdriver?

35) What is the difference between a Ramos Fizz and a Silver Fizz?

36) How would olives be stored?

37) Name four rules of etiquette pertaining to a bartender's posture and manner.

38) How should celery be stored?

39) What is the difference between a Greyhound and a Salty Dog?

40) Name one type of rye whiskey.

41) What are the four steps to using a jigger?

42) Why is it best to never use the same ice twice when using a mixing glass?

43) What is meant by the term breakage?

44) Why should each customer be greeted with a smile?

45) How long can lime wheels be stored?

46) What is the difference between a Tom Collins and a John Collins?

47) Name three popular premium call liquors.

48) If you're right handed, what should you learn to pour with your left hand?

49) Name three brands of Canadian whisky.

50) Name ten primary cocktails.